Printed in Canada.

Contact
hello@alabasterco.com
www.alabasterco.com

Alabaster Co. The Bible Beautiful.
Visual imagery & thoughtful design integrated within the Bible.
Cultivating conversation between art, beauty, & faith.

Founded in 2016.

 ALABASTER

The Good and Beautiful

Bible Study

VOL. I

An Introduction &
How to use this book

The Bible is good and beautiful. Its vast, historical recognition not only establishes its authority in our collective lives, but also shows us how its story and storytellers lead us to something bigger than ourselves.

Hearing stories has always deepened our understanding of our world. In early Jewish traditions, we see storytelling as a foundation for the flourishing of relationships, knowledge, and culture. Deuteronomy 11 (NLT) invites its audience to "commit yourselves wholeheartedly to these words" and "Talk about them when you are at home and when you are on the road, when you are going to bed and when you are getting up." These early traditions invite us to hear stories as an enduring, generational, and immersive experience.

This invitation from Biblical storytellers is often overlooked in our modern society. In today's contexts, it can be easy to reduce this ancient text to a set of brief take-aways, or moral to-do lists. But when we choose to see the Bible in this way we miss out on the fullness of what these stories can be—something wholly sensory and embodied.

We can look to early traditions of storytelling as a guide to engaging with the Bible today. The first communities gathered around sacred Bible stories, learning to embody those stories from generation to generation. Art has played a prominent part in this process, transmitting biblical stories and making them meaningful for each new generation. There is wisdom in following the steps of this method—noting how things transpire, and allowing them to speak, without rush or force. We used this as a guide in designing *The Good and Beautiful Bible Study* and invite you to engage with it two-fold:

READ

Whether it's heard aloud or in silent reading, hearing the story in its presented form is a bedrock for curiosity, conversation, and relationship.

I.

Each chapter's reading section opens with a **designated theme**, **synopsis**, and **reading list**. We invite you to begin your chapter experience by investigating these resources.

II.

The chapter then has an **outline**, retelling the story's events. To conclude the readings, we move into the **today** section, where we ponder the story and inspect its qualities and themes as they exist in our modern world today.

REFLECT

Through thoughtful curation of artwork, guided prompts, questions, and design, we invite you to integrate the story into the present and embody a full sensory experience. Looking to early traditions, we encourage gathering and sharing in this experience with others.

Each chapter's reflect section is structured with prompts that will guide you through a process: Pause, Ponder, and Pray.

I.

Pause: Bring awareness to your response to the story. Each chapter has contemplative artwork and prompts inspired by the story's theme(s) to help guide you into the following steps below.

II.

Ponder: Deepen your understanding of the story with questions to reflect and/or discuss with your community.

III.

Pray: Close your time with a written prayer uniquely crafted for each chapter.

We hope these promptings and works of art allow for a deeper experience with the Bible. Through your study, let there be joy, kinship, and an abounding connection with goodness and all of creation. Amen.

Vol. I

Need

The
5000

Need

The Story of The 5000

SYNOPSIS

A large crowd from various communities hurries together to seek Jesus; Jesus perceives and tends to their holistic needs.

KEY MOMENT:
Mark 6:30-43

Read

OUTLINE

Perhaps it starts as a small trickle of people, picking up steam with each new town they pass. Eventually, like a crowd of marathon runners, they are jogging in a large, unruly pack of thousands.[1]

While some English translations say they "hurried,"[2] the original Greek uses a word that could be translated as "they ran together" or "they rushed together." They are running together—people from different towns and different families, people with different occupations and life experiences and personalities—united only by their urgent need to be where Jesus is.

They know they need something from Jesus. They recognize Jesus getting away in his boat, and they waste no time setting off on foot in pursuit.

What exactly did they need?

First, the crowd needs compassion. When Jesus reaches the other side of the lake, he sees the crowd and has *loving-pity* for them.[3] In Greek that's a strong word—literally, Jesus is *moved to the bowels*.

Jesus is moved because he sees that the crowd needs all the things sheep need from a shepherd:[4] guidance, wisdom, direction, safety. They need protection from their predators, who are many—from occupying Roman armies, to predatory money-lenders and tax collectors, to corrupt religious leadership.

NEED

The crowd also needs teaching. They hurry around the lake to meet Jesus because they know they need to hear what he has to say. They are hungry to know how to live. They are starving for peace and wholeness in a violent world; for justice in an unjust world. And so Jesus teaches them.

Perhaps the crowd is so transfixed by Jesus' story-telling that, as day begins to fade to evening, they hardly realize they are hungry for food. Perhaps they have not been able to carry much with them on their long jog around the lake. Most are very materially poor; perhaps many don't know where their next meal is coming from.

The disciples ask Jesus to send the crowd away to buy dinner for themselves. But Jesus understands needs are not just spiritual or emotional; they are tangible and material as well. He asks the disciples to feed the crowd themselves. It is a baffling instruction; they hardly have money for a feat like that.[5]

But Jesus isn't concerned about the resources they don't have. Instead, he wants to help the whole community find and share what they *do* have. The disciples survey the crowd and report back: five loaves, two fish.[6]

Jesus gives thanks to God for these communal resources, scant as they may seem. As Jesus breaks the bread and asks his disciples to distribute it to the people, the miracle happens. The bread is not running out, and neither is the fish.

[5] Mark 6:35-37 / [6] Mark 6:38

Everyone is eating, and everyone has plenty.[7] In the Greek, they are *filled to the full*. They are satisfied completely. Their needs are met with surprising, miraculous, communal abundance.

And perhaps this is the one last thing the crowd needs. They need to know that, with God, everyone eats to the full—truly, everyone—and there are plenty of leftovers.[8] At God's table everything is shared, and everyone's needs are seen and provided for. At God's banquet there is no need to compete, no need to push and shove to be first in line for food. There is only an invitation to sit down, rest, and let God provide. The God of Jesus is a God who meets human need with divine abundance.

NEED

Jesus cares about the entire, holistic needs of people. Today, just as in Jesus' time, many people have needs that go beyond just the spiritual; they have serious material needs too—the need for comfortable and affordable housing, the need for a car, the need for health care, the need for work that pays a livable wage. Jesus doesn't just callously tell people not to worry about these things; rather he meets these needs as part of caring for the whole human being. He takes tangible steps to make sure no one goes hungry.

As Danté Stewart writes in *Shoutin' in the Fire: An American Epistle:* "When Jesus healed people, he wasn't just concerned about their souls. He was concerned about their bodies. Bodies caught up in oppression and exploitation. Bodies forgotten by the community and the empire. Bodies caught up in the streets." Jesus cares about *whole* people—and about all people. He cares about the people our society tends to overlook and undervalue.

If God is a God who meets human need with divine abundance, what does that look like in our communities? Who isn't experiencing this abundance? What are the barriers that keep them from it, and what would it look like for those barriers to be removed? We are united at God's banquet table by our common neediness. Our needs are part of our humanity; they are nothing to be ashamed of. We are meant to care for others and be cared for by others in healthy, interdependent communities. Across the world, mutual aid networks are doing just that. Ordinary people are coming together in creative and cooperative ways to meet one another's needs.

How aware are we of our needs? How willing are we to share our needs with others? What might it look like to bravely and vulnerably name our needs in all forms—and to support others as they do the same?

Yoshino
KAMISAKA SEKKA, 1909-1910   **INK AND COLOR ON PAPER**

Reflect

PAUSE

Sit up straight.

Take a deep breath.

Using the art element (on the previous page), take a moment to reflect on the story.

PONDER

Invite God to speak to you:

I.

What is your reaction to the thought of expressing your needs? What does it look like to be open to others caring for your needs?

II.

How aware are we of the needs of those around us? Are there people in our society that we may overlook? How can we learn their needs better?

III.

How does the feeling of scarcity prohibit us from helping each other? How does Jesus show us that there is abundance today?

PRAY

God of Abundance,
help us to believe
that you meet the needs of all.
When our bodies grumble,
and our legs are tired,
may we rest together
and be filled to the full.
Amen.

Decisive Action / Subverting Expectations / Non-Violence

Abigail

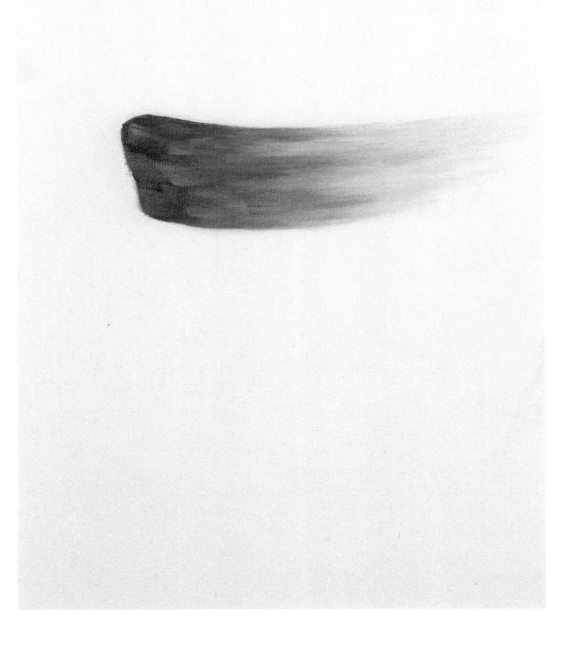

The Story of Abigail

SYNOPSIS

Abigail is an overlooked hero who takes decisive, subversive action against the violent acts of those around her to save the lives of many.

KEY MOMENT:
1 Samuel 25

Read

OUTLINE

Abigail's story is set within David's nomadic journey to the throne. David, with a sizeable army in Carmel, encounters sheep being sheared. These sheep are the property of Nabal, Abigail's husband. David and his men remain with the flock and the shepherds, protecting all of Nabal's property with their presence. In return, David asks Nabal for provisions for his army, an expected courtesy for such protection.[1]

Nabal responds with more than a refusal; he insults David. Ignoring the act of kindness given to him by such an imposing army, Nabal dismisses David as a nobody and returns to feasting.[2]

David's anger flares up in a call to arms. He leaves a third of his army to protect their baggage while the others prepare to confront Nabal and slaughter his entire household.[3]

Abigail is informed of the coming attack and springs into action. Quickly, she has a gift assembled to appease David but does not inform her husband. Wine and bread, dressed sheep and extra grain, raisins and figs—all are loaded on donkeys and sent off to the coming army with Abigail following closely behind.[4] Perhaps this is a risk she takes knowing that likely her husband expects her to stay behind and support his decisions. Perhaps she is more keenly aware that violence is coming. To Abigail, saving lives was more important than staying in her lane. She bends expectations for a greater good.

So here comes the wife of Nabal, instead of Nabal himself. When she meets David, Abigail takes responsibility for her husband's brashness and lack of

[1] 1 Samuel 25:4-6 / [2] 1 Samuel 25:10-11 / [3] 1 Samuel 25:13 / [4] 1 Samuel 25:18-19

hospitality—although she had nothing to do with it! She acts on behalf of her husband, more than making up for his failure.

Abigail could simply have sent the gift and hoped for the best. But her actions show recognition for what David will become: the next king of Israel. In that moment, Abigail acts in spite of fear and violence, and in the midst of poor decisions made by others. Abigail's pleading for peace shows discernment and foresight.

David applauds her good sense and quick thinking, recognizing that she kept him from violence and releases her back to her household in peace. The worst is over; tempers fizzle out and she has saved many lives.

Abigail returns to find her husband still feasting, unaware that death came knocking on his door. She decides to leave him in ignorance until morning. When she tells him what has happened, Nabal's shock is great and within ten days he dies.[5]

On his journeys, David hears of Nabal's death, and he sends for Abigail to be his wife. Abigail consents to the marriage and joins him on his way to the throne.[6]

TODAY

Abigail's impact surmounts how little she is mentioned in the Bible. In a culture obsessed with celebrity, renown, and prestige, Abigail reminds us it is most often overlooked heroes who make our world a better place. Her story encourages us to act wherever we find ourselves, even when it means coloring outside the lines. She commanded authority without being given it explicitly (by her role in society as a woman). She saw a need and took necessary action to prevent destruction, even when it meant subverting the norms.

[5] 1 Samuel 25:36-38 / [6] 1 Samuel 25:42

Abigail's story also teaches us *how* to take decisive action. So often, when met with an oppositional force, our tendency is towards violence. This might not be physical violence outright, however, as Dr. Marshall B. Rosenberg defines it in his book, *Non-Violent Communication:*

"If 'violent' means acting in ways that result in hurt or harm, then much of how we communicate—judging others, bullying, having racial bias, blaming, finger pointing, discriminating, speaking without listening, criticizing others or ourselves, name-calling, reacting when angry, using political rhetoric, being defensive or judging who's 'good/bad' or what's 'right/wrong' with people—could indeed be called 'violent communication.'"

Such is the violent and rash reactions of Nabal and David. Abigail's swift and decisive actions demonstrate the complete opposite of them. Instead of inciting violence, she gives. Instead of brashness, she demonstrates listening and intentionality. Instead of hostility, she shows hospitality.

Abigail's story asks us to think about the ways we choose to respond to people around us. If the problem is beyond our apparent influence, should we just stick to our roles—or do we choose to take decisive action? And how do we take action—do we move in opposition to others, or do we subvert expectations, non-violently, to serve a greater good?

Confluence
BRYAN YE-CHUNG, 2022　　　　　　　　　　　　　　　　OIL ON CANVAS

DECISIVE ACTION / SUBVERTING EXPECTATIONS

Reflect

PAUSE

Sit up straight.

Take a deep breath.

Using the art element (on the previous page),
take a moment to reflect on the story.

PONDER

Invite God to speak to you:

I.

Where do you see yourself in Abigail's story?
What parts can you relate to?

II.

Are there areas in your life that require swift, decisive
action even though it might be subverting norms?

III.

What challenges you about non-violent communication? In the face of opposition how can you respond non-violently?

PRAY

God,
you see my motives, hurts, and dreams.
Help me to see beyond
what I can see on the outside,
even if that means bending expectations.
Help me to watch for unexpected moments,
for chances to be bold,
and to act decisively.
May these moments of boldness
and action be in the service of *Shalom*.
Amen.

Boy Jesus

The Story of Boy Jesus

SYNOPSIS

We explore the story of Jesus as a child and what it looks like to love and honor our families while faithfully pursuing the unique path God has for us.

KEY MOMENT:
Luke 2:41-52

Read

This story provides us with a rare glimpse into Jesus' childhood. While his birth is documented in great detail, we know little about his upbringing outside of this account. However, it's a vignette rich with insight into a growing Messiah. At twelve years old, we see him discovering his divine calling—much to the confusion of his earthly parents.

Mary and Joseph endured many challenges since the birth of their son, from living as refugees in Egypt to facing the lingering stigma of a pregnancy that preceded marriage. But Jesus' parents remained devout throughout, circumcising him on the eighth day and bringing him to the temple for purification after childbirth. On the latter visit, both Simeon and Anna prophesied over the infant Messiah, filling their hearts with wonder and curiosity about his mysterious future.

Until then, though, what would it be like to raise God?

Years later, in today's passage, we find preteen Jesus accompanying his family on their annual trip to Jerusalem for the Passover festival. They make the grueling pilgrimage on foot, traveling in a caravan with other family and community members. We can surmise Jesus is a social kid because his parents assume he is walking with the other travelers on the first day's journey home. But when he doesn't turn up at nightfall, they start to panic.[1]

Three days of frantic searching pass before they find their son in an unusual circumstance: sitting cross-legged in the temple court, surrounded by religious scholars. For three days, he has been listening and learning and asking questions about scripture. The

[1] Luke 2:42-45

leaders spoke with awe of their son's wisdom and understanding beyond his years.[2]

Relieved and angry, they scold Jesus for the anxiety he has caused. His response is one of innocent confusion: "Why were you searching for me? Didn't you know I had to be in my Father's house?"[3] To him, it seems obvious. After all, his parents are the ones who raised him to love God and revere his commands. Why didn't they know to check the temple first? And shouldn't they be proud?

Even at this young age, Jesus can feel a special connection to God. He stays behind simply because he wants to be close to his heavenly Father. However, we can only imagine the rejection his parents may have felt to hear him say this. Despite all the prophecies spoken over him, he is still their son whom they loved ever since he was a crying baby. In this jarring interaction, he becomes a mystery to them again.

This incident foreshadows the many times in Jesus' ministry when he would be misunderstood. Religious leaders would accuse him, crowds would scorn him, and even his disciples would struggle to comprehend him. After a particularly disappointing visit to Nazareth, he would remark that "a prophet is honored everywhere except in his own hometown and among his relatives and his own family."[4]

But Jesus never wavered in his calling. Instead, he returned again and again to his Father's presence, just as he had as a little boy of twelve years old.

[2]Luke 2:46-47 / [3]Luke 2:49 NIV / [4]Mark 6:4 NIV

It's comforting to note that Jesus understands what it's like to be born into a family. This story reminds us that every parent has dreams for their children and every child longs to make their parents proud. But as we grow, tension naturally begins to build between family expectations and the inescapable reality of who we are.

For those of us who come from a legacy of faith, this process may be complicated by a desire to explore our beliefs in a way that varies from how our parents express theirs. For others, conflicts may arise from where we choose to work, who we choose to be with, or how we choose to spend our time. It can be bewildering when parents become distressed by our very efforts to live out the values they instilled in us. What do we do when God leads us in a seemingly contradictory direction?

With so many voices in our ears from this noisy world— from peers and religious mentors to secular leaders we admire—it's tempting to fixate on the approval of people we respect while missing God's whispers to us in the process. It feels much safer to go along with what's familiar than to embrace the tension of our own journey with Jesus into the wilderness.

As we make our lives our own, it's equally important to acknowledge the wisdom our parents and mentors passed down to us, and to identify the new territory God may be calling us to explore. Every family must navigate this process of respecting one another while recognizing God has a unique story for each of us. May we honor each person's pilgrimage as we consistently return to where we all belong: our Father's house.

Mount Lagrev

CARL ALBERT VON SALIS

OIL ON CANVAS

Reflect

Sit up straight.

Take a deep breath.

Using the art element (on the previous page),
take a moment to reflect on the story.

PONDER

Invite God to speak to you:

I.

What expectations have you experienced from your
family growing up? How have you navigated them?

II.

Who has been a source of wisdom in your life?
What wisdom have they passed down to you?

III.

In what areas of your life do you feel invited to explore your own story? How can you make space in
your life to do it?

PRAY

God of all things new,
thank you for watching over me.
For sending those to walk before me,
that I may find my own story.
Teach me to honor and love
the pilgrimage of many.
In your name,
Amen.

The Canaanite Woman

The Story of the Canaanite Woman

SYNOPSIS

A Canaanite woman displays agency and persistency as she goes to Jesus in need of healing.

AGENCY / PERSISTENCY

KEY MOMENT:	FULL READING:
Matthew 15:21-28	Matthew 15:21-31

Read

OUTLINE

The story begins with Jesus withdrawing to the regions of Tyre and Sidon during his busy time in ministry. There, a woman comes out to him and shouts with anguish, "Lord, Son of David, have mercy on me! My daughter is demon-possessed and suffering terribly!"[1]

The cry of this woman emerges from a deep love and care for her daughter. Her cry is deep; it is a cry laced with faith. The faith of this woman is evident from the beginning as she places her body in a dangerous situation, knowing all the harmful implications that could occur in this culture. Being a Gentile woman amongst a group of Jewish men, she is crossing a social boundary by speaking up to a group with more cultural power than she has. Initially, she is met with silence. The silence holds within it her hopes, fears, and anxiousness. Filled with emotion and faith, she persists, so much so that the disciples beg Jesus to send her away.[2]

Jesus finally addresses the woman, and we are caught off guard as he reinforces the line of exclusion saying, "I was sent only to the lost sheep of Israel."[3]

The woman is blocked in a way anyone whose prayers have gone unanswered might feel blocked. And yet, the woman feels the weight of the line and chooses to cross it anyway. She kneels before him and calls him Lord, indicating his lordship over even her.

Surely Jesus will answer her wish now! No, his reply is even harsher than before, "It is not right to take the children's bread and toss it to the dogs."[4] Jesus appears not only to reinforce the line he drew, but he builds a wall, and renders the mother to the likes of a dog.

AGENCY / PERSISTENCY

---

[1] Matthew 15:22 NIV / [2] Matthew 15:23 / [3] Matthew 15:24 NIV / [4] Matthew 15:26 NIV

Anyone else would've taken the hint, for the insult must have been felt acutely. Perhaps her breath got shallow, her hands shaking, her forehead full with sweat. But still, the woman refuses to be excluded. "Even the dogs eat the crumbs that fall from their master's table."[5]

While filled with the trauma of the experience, the woman refuses to allow silence, or separation, or being equated to an animal stop her from what she knows she deserves. For this, she is rewarded. Jesus replies, "Woman you have great faith! Your request is granted."[6] The woman's daughter is healed immediately.

The Canaanite woman's narrative displays the important role of agency and persistency in interacting with God. It was ultimately her push back against a block, for the sake of her family, that resulted in healing.

How many of us feel we can push back against God? Too often our interactions with God are the opposite—quietly passive and submissive. But this is not the type of partnership God invites us into. The woman's story reminds us all that we have agency when interacting with God. We can go to God in desperation; we can have friction; we can tussle—this is the stuff of real relationships. It may not be effective at first; it may even feel as if our dignity is being disrespected, despite our sincerity. But the woman's story shows us that our agency in shaping our relationship with God can lead to healing—even in the face of a door that God initially says is closed. This is ultimately a process that leads to liberation.

[5] Matthew 15:27 NIV / [6] Matthew 15:28 NIV

The story does not tell us why Jesus rejected the woman, or why he played into cultural exclusions. Nevertheless, the story shows us that God does not desire our passivity, but instead God leads us into spaces of partnership.

The clearest invitation to this kind of relationship between God and God's people is found in the name Israel. In Hebrew, *Israel* can be translated as "wrestles (or struggles) with God." The Canaanite woman knew that the God of Israel is a God who invites this kind of engagement and participation. Against cultural expectations, she embodied the spirit of God's people as she engaged Jesus in this messy yet beautiful moment.

This Canaanite woman exemplifies the reality that we don't achieve healing fully on our own, but we are invited to participate and partner with God in our own healing. As we do participate, we experience a type of liberation that acknowledges we have a voice and agency within our mutual relationship with God. We can trust God will meet us in our breath, in our fight, and in our struggle—even in our struggle with God.

Wrestlers
JULIA SIGNE, 2021   OIL ON FOUND FABRIC

Reflect

Sit up straight.

Take a deep breath.

Using the art element (on the previous page), take a moment to reflect on the story.

PONDER Invite God to speak to you:

I. Where have you felt a lack of agency in your faith life? Where did those barriers come from?

II. When have you come to God with a request, only for it to go unfulfilled? What does it look like to push back with even more faith?

PRAY God of Israel,
I come to you again for healing.
May I never let go.
May faith cross all barriers,
and liberation abound here and now.
Amen.

The Daughters of Zelophehad

The Story of the Daughters of Zelophehad

SYNOPSIS

This little-known story takes place when the Daughters of Zelophehad find themselves with no inheritance and with no resources but each other. They advocate for their needs and change a law for the better.

> **KEY MOMENT:**
> Numbers 27:1-11

Read

OUTLINE

After a traumatic and awe-inspiring exodus from slavery under the Egyptians, the Israelites find themselves wandering the Sinai wilderness in search of a promise—a home where they can finally trade roaming for rest.

At this point in their story, the Israelites had been through uprisings and rebellions, conflicts both internally and with other peoples, encounters with enemy kings and hostile deities. But the heart of their journey hinges on an important question: what does it mean to be in community with each other?

We meet sisters Mahlah, Noah, Hoglah, Micah and Tirzah in this setting. Recently bereaved of their father Zelophehad, they face an anxious dilemma as unmarried women in a patrilineal system that legally requires male heirs for the transfer of wealth and property. They stand to lose everything because their father has no sons.

But the sisters recognize that their needs for safety, security, and resources for survival would be best met by their father's inheritance. The alternative would be to rely on the generosity of their extended family while waiting for their own marriages. However, that would also mean that their father's name would end with his death.

So the sisters take matters into their own hands.

In the presence of Moses, the priests, the leaders, and the congregation of the Israelites, they openly question the Levitical Law set by God and delivered through Moses. They ask, "Why should the name of our father be taken away from his clan because he had no son? Give to us a possession among our father's brothers."[1]

There is no guarantee they would have made it out of that situation unharmed. There are plenty of Old Testament examples of people whom God strikes down for disrespect or disobedience. Their request to retain the inheritance of their father is a direct challenge to the parameters God had set for the community.

Moses presents their case before God, and God affirms that the sisters are *right* to bring their petition and agrees to meet their need.[2] God does not simply make a special exception, but further instructs Moses to change the law itself in order to meet the evolving needs of the community. From that point on, "if a man dies and has no son, then give his inheritance on to his daughters,"[3] God commands.

These sisters took account of their needs and found the determination to advocate for themselves in a system that was not created to consider them. And not only did they get their needs met and change the system for themselves, but it was also changed for those that came after them.

TODAY

It may come as a surprise that a book like Numbers—tucked away between genealogies, legal code and ritual requirements for worship—would invite us to consider what it means to advocate for our needs in a communal space.

As modern readers, we may not quite see just how brave these sisters' actions were at face value. Advocating for their needs as women without the support of a man was a brave act in a patriarchal commu-

[1] Numbers 27:4 / [2] Numbers 27:7 / [3] Numbers 27:8

nity. While our surroundings may be different than Mahlah, Noah, Hoglah, Micah and Tirzah, many of us confront similar obstacles in a world that often demands we find the courage to speak or to act on behalf of ourselves.

We may feel a deep conviction inside us, but find that conviction is unwelcome in certain spaces we inhabit. Depending on who we are and where we are, we may find certain powers and principalities would prefer us to be silent and disconnected from our own voice and our own needs.

Yet our world craves examples of those who choose to nurture and connect to their own needs. It's too easy to stay disconnected from our inner voice and allow certain norms to dictate our futures. But those who remain attentive to their own needs, like the sisters in this story, have the opportunity to forge their own path forward—a path that others can follow.

Working out our needs in community does not mean that our advocacy comes with immediate results. It is hard work. It does not always come in the form we expect. It takes time, effort and grit to see it through. At times it may feel constrained by forces bent on keeping us insecure and overwhelmed. Yet we are called by God's voice to know ourselves and know others in community as we ask for what we need.

This little known story from Numbers reminds us that when we find ourselves in unfavorable community spaces, choosing to advocate for ourselves anyways might yield results we do not expect. Learning to advocate for our needs can not only change our circumstances for the better, but also provide for the needs of those who come after us. Like the sisters, perhaps it is when we choose to advocate for what we need in community that we have the greatest impact.

On Land and Sea: Land
DEA JENKINS, 2020
WATERCOLOR ON PAPER

Reflect

Sit up straight.

Take a deep breath.

Using the art element (on the previous page),
take a moment to reflect on the story.

Invite God to speak to you:

I.

Have there been times in your life when you have gone from neglecting your needs to connecting to them? What does it look like to connect to your needs, and then advocate for them?

II.

Do you have a community in which you share resources, needs, and take actions together? Where do you find these communities?

III.

How do today's systems and constructs not meet our needs (physical, spiritual, emotional), and how do we meet them for ourselves and our communities?

God who sees, would you see us when
our needs are not met.
God who hears, would you hear us when
we advocate for ourselves and each other.
Empower us to make new things happen
so your people can live fully and freely.
Amen.

CONNECTING TO OUR NEEDS

Bravery

Deborah

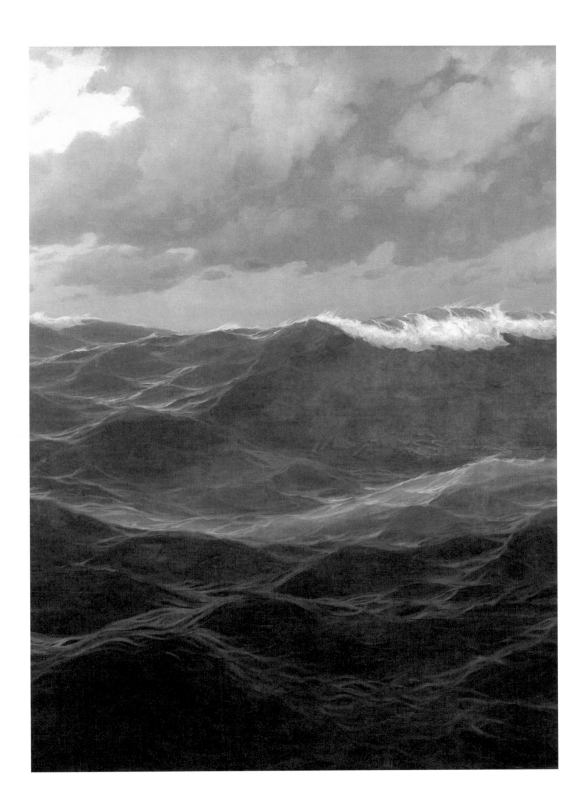

The Story of Deborah

BRAVERY

SYNOPSIS

As a brave prophet, Deborah guides the people of Israel from the front lines of a battle to end their suffering.

KEY MOMENT:	FULL READING:
Judges 4:4-24	Judges 4-5

Read

OUTLINE

The story picks up in a time where the people of Israel forego their commitment to live in step with God. Choosing this straying path—evil over love, selfishness instead of mercy—leads them to suffer under the oppressive rule of King Jabin and his commander Sisera.[1]

In this time comes the prophet and leader, Deborah. Deborah's role in her community was to speak wisdom into situations of injustice. Day after day, she'd sit under a large palm tree, and tend to men and women seeking wisdom and sound judgment.[2]

One day, Deborah summons the military commander Barak, relaying God's message to prepare for battle and to gather the troops. It was time for the people to break free and fight Sisera's army!

The enormity of the situation overwhelms Barak; while he trusts Deborah, he wants her to go with him to rally the troops. "If you go with me, I will go; but if you don't go with me, I won't go."[3] Deborah bravely says she will, but also calls out Barak's wavering spirit and responds with a prophetic promise—it won't be him, but "the hands of a woman"[4] who will defeat Sisera.

Barak and Deborah begin to gather a large army to wage battle for the flourishing of their people. Word gets back to Sisera that they are preparing for battle, so Sisera gathers nine hundred iron chariots. Deborah strategically tells Barak to get ready, knowing that, by the grace of God, this oppressive army will lead themselves right where Barak needs them. She is full of assured confidence in God, telling Barak: "Go! This is the day the Lord has given Sisera into your hands. Has not the Lord gone ahead of you?"[5]

BRAVERY

And that's exactly what happens. The armies of Israel are given prime opportunity to strike. Victory is theirs. No soldier from Sisera's army is spared, and Sisera himself *flees*, running for his life and taking shelter within the tent of one of his nation's allies—Heber and his wife, Jael.

Jael welcomes him and agrees not to alert anyone. That night, Sisera falls asleep and seeing an opportunity, Jael kills him by driving a tent peg through his temple.[6] Thus, she fulfills Deborah's prophecy to Barak—a woman's hand will kill Sisera.

Deborah and Barak celebrate! A joyous song is sung to usher in forty years of peace in the land, and is etched into history as one of the oldest written excerpts of Scripture.

TODAY

Like Deborah, we too are invited to be people of bravery even amidst insurmountable odds. She had every reason to have doubts—whether it was the 900 iron chariots lined before her, having to deal with intense quarrels among her people, or needing to garner command over numerous men in power. But instead of fear, Deborah exemplifies the complete opposite. She *exudes* confidence and authority as she boldly listens to God, wielding her courage to free her people.

We are reminded of many leaders of the civil rights movement rooted in these qualities, like Fannie Lou Hamer. As a devoted faith leader and Black woman in the 1960s South, Fannie Lou Hamer was part of a marginalized community living under oppressive and racist systems and structures. Though she was threatened, arrested, and subject to violence, it never deterred her from her life's work. She was brave,

[6] Judges 4:21

continually putting her body on the line with civil acts of disobedience to expose inequities and inequalities.

When dire times call for bravery, how do we respond? God does not leave us, even when we are most afraid. We can trust that the Spirit will empower us in truth and righteousness when we need to be brave. Barak wavered to rally the troops—but Deborah was there, ready, trusting God—and so was Jael. Contrast Barak's trepidation with Deborah's confidence. As she commands Barak she says: "Has not the Lord gone ahead of you?" Such a rhetorical question reveals her assuredness in God, and she gets to experience that assuredness fully realized in victory.

When we choose fear we miss out on opportunities in life; we shrink and diminish below what God intends for us. But when we choose bravery we get to live in step with God and experience the fullness that life has to offer. What is stirring your soul, spurring you on to act bravely? Be brave; perhaps it will lead to a wondrous chorus.

Großes Marinestück
MAX JENSEN, 1880

OIL ON CANVAS

Reflect

Sit up straight.

Take a deep breath.

Using the art element (on the previous page),
take a moment to reflect on the story.

PONDER

Invite God to speak to you:

I.

Where are you invited to be brave? How can you
rise to God's call for bravery?

II.

What stirs your soul and makes you sing? How can
it help you live bravely?

III.

How can we wield our courage from God to bring
freedom to ourselves and others?

PRAY

You alone, God, are my strength.
Each step with You
my soul is stirred and my heart sings.
Grant me bravery
when I am faced with hardships.
And may I join in
the divine melody of life
with You.
Amen.

Waiting With Hope

Elizabeth

The Story of Elizabeth

SYNOPSIS

While experiencing great pressures and challenges amidst her maternal journey, Elizabeth waits with hope and expectation for the fulfillment of her desire to have a child.

> **KEY MOMENT:**
> Luke 1

Read

Luke begins the story by elevating the character of Elizabeth and her husband Zachariah. Both are described as righteous before God, "careful to obey all the commandments and regulations."[1] Yet, they deal with the uncomfortable reality of barrenness, which in Jewish culture was commonly viewed as an indicator of personal sin and punishment from God (i.e. Lev 20:20). In Elizabeth's old age, with no physical signs of conceiving, she carried that stigma every day. But despite co-existing in the tension of being both blameless and childless, she lived a faith-filled life, quietly holding the desire of one day bearing a child close to her heart for many years.

Then one day, unexpectedly, her husband comes home mute after encountering the angel Gabriel who prophesies they will have a son.[2] A son who will be a great prophet, filled with the Holy Spirit and who will set the stage for the coming Messiah. Soon after, Elizabeth actually conceives this foretold baby and spends five months in seclusion.[3]

Why choose seclusion upon hearing this blessed news? Was she waiting for her pregnancy to be visible to the rest of the world as a physical sign? Was she spending her time undistracted, in prayer and praise with God? Though it's uncertain, Elizabeth, just like the many years before she conceived, continued to wait.

In the sixth month of Elizabeth's pregnancy, her cousin Mary also has an encounter with the angel Gabriel who tells her she will miraculously conceive Jesus. When Mary goes to visit Elizabeth, the moment Mary's voice meets Elizabeth's ears, her baby leaps

[1] Luke 1:6 / [2] Luke 1:19-20 / [3] Luke 1:24

in the womb. The Holy Spirit fills Elizabeth with joy and she pronounces a blessing. With Elizabeth's testimony present and fully showing in her rounded belly, the Holy Spirit gives her the ability to immediately recognize the similar favor God has bestowed upon Mary—to carry the One all of Israel has been waiting for. Elizabeth is filled with a sured hope that the end of waiting to see her Messiah is on the horizon.[4]

Elizabeth's waiting is met with a fulfilled promise—a child they name John (whom we come to know as John the Baptist). Her community, the ones that previously shunned and shamed her, gathered around to rejoice with her in this miraculous event.

TODAY

Waiting is not easy. Waiting with hope is an even more difficult task when faced with seemingly impossible circumstances. But it is a virtue that keeps our spirits alive and ready to receive when our desires are finally fulfilled.

Elizabeth's display of waiting with hope reminds us of the stories of many people who find themselves wrongfully shamed, blamed, or physically shunned. In 1992, Ray Krone was sentenced to prison for a murder he did not commit. He spent a total of 10 years moving around different Arizona prisons and 32 months on death row. In 2002, when a DNA test was finally conducted, Krone was found innocent. On the day of his release, Krone's mother was conversing with a reporter, remarking that every

[4] Luke 1:39-45

Thanksgiving and Christmas their family would set a place at the table for Ray, waiting patiently for him to come home. While Krone's physical circumstances appeared highly unfavorable, his mother held onto the hope that her son would be found innocent and eventually released; and so he was.

In her waiting, Elizabeth served God, and even secluded herself until her pregnancy began to show; and in the same way Ray's mother set a place at the table for him every year. Both individuals did not know how their stories would end, but it didn't prevent them from holding onto the possibility of their desires coming to fruition.

We all have things we are waiting for. Elizabeth's story is an invitation to wait—not with pessimism, cynicism, or negativity—but full of hope knowing the God of fulfillment is with us.

Moonscape
ERIC TAI, 2021   OYSTERSHELL ON CANVAS

Reflect

PAUSE

Sit up straight.

Take a deep breath.

Using the art element (on the previous page),
take a moment to reflect on the story.

PONDER

Invite God to speak to you:

I.

What are you waiting for most adamantly? What
role does hope have in your waiting?

II.

Where is God in your waiting? How do you spend
your time with God when you are waiting?

III.

When have you kept your time of waiting between
just you and God? When have you invited community into your time of waiting?

PRAY

God who is beyond time,
help me to wait faithfully
and remain hopeful.
For you can do all things
even when they feel insurmountable.
May I seek you when I wait for you,
may I seek community
in the waiting,
and celebrate with others.
Amen.

Courage / God's Providence

Esther

The Story of Esther

SYNOPSIS

The story of Esther is about a woman whose life was caught up in circumstances and traumas bigger than herself, who acted with courage to save her people—and amidst it all shines a light on a God working behind the scenes.

KEY MOMENT:	**FULL READING:**
Esther 4-7	Esther 1-10

Read

Esther's story was historically conceived to recount the significance of the Jewish festival, Purim. *Purim* can be translated to "lots", a form of decision-making that appears to be made by chance. This quality shapes much of the story of Esther, celebrating the mysterious intermingling of chance and divine providence.

The story begins with Esther being plucked out from under the care of her uncle, Mordecai, and placed in the fortress of Susa, getting prepared to be presented to King Xerxes as a potential wife.[1] The "preparation" is traumatic—she has no choice and no authority in the circumstance; and, Mordecai, aware that her Jewish nationality could put her in danger in the king's courts, advises her to keep her heritage a secret. So there she is, without her family, disconnected from her own people, and without any choice—being presented (amongst many other women) to King Xerxes.

To everyone's surprise, King Xerxes not only favors Esther, but makes her the queen. What are the odds?

Here in the story we're introduced to another character, Haman, who is promoted as the most powerful official in the empire.[2] After a tense encounter and feeling disrespected by Mordecai, Haman hatches a plot to destroy the Jewish people. He brings his plan to the king, alleging the Jewish people refuse to follow the king's laws. King Xerxes agrees with Haman and signs a decree, declaring a day in the future as the day all of the Jewish people in the Persian Empire should be killed.

Where is Esther in all of this?

COURAGE / GOD'S PROVIDENCE

Well, she's unaware the decree was signed. When she hears her uncle Mordecai is in distress, she sends to find out why.[3] She finds out her people, who are courageously resisting their captivity, are now set to be killed by the king. In step with the spirit of her community, she conceives of a plan to resist this order, but it would require her to willingly put herself in danger in the court—no one, including the queen, is allowed to enter the king's court uninvited. Seeing the dangerous circumstances in front of her, Esther asks Mordecai to gather their people to fast and pray for her, as she prepares to present herself before the king.

While her people are fasting, Esther devises a plan to set up a situation where she can persuade the king to save her people, incriminating Haman in the process. During the second feast she requests, while they were all drinking wine, Esther reveals it is her people that are set to be killed, and that Haman instigated it all.[4]

Esther, in that moment, risks her life by identifying herself as a member of the people set to be killed. She chances vulnerability in the hope it would change the mind of the king. And it does. The story ends on a triumphant note, with her uncle Mordecai being put into a position of power and her people gaining the right to fight for themselves.[5]

Esther began this story in a place of trauma. She had no choice, no authority, and was disconnected from her people. The odds were stacked against her and her community. But this story ends with a resilient tone. Though her people still faced many challenges of captivity, her commitment to her community saved the lives of her people—keeping them from experiencing a collective trauma—death.

Where is God in all of this?

In all of its twists and turns, God goes unmentioned in the story. This might seem strange at first—for something within the Biblical canon—but here lies its brilliance. Through all its twists, turns, and chance-filled moments, lies a picture of God—working behind the scenes, setting up salvation of the Jewish people.

[3] Esther 4 / [4] Esther 7 / [5] Esther 8

Looking to Esther as a guide, we see courage is something that simultaneously takes vulnerability, community, and time. This story reminds us of all of the communities faced with injustice in recent history who turned to their own for support. Over many years, women with Esther's qualities courageously fought to gain the right to vote in the United States in the '20s; and in the civil rights movement in the '50s and '60s, many Black Americans organized their communities, fighting for a more inclusive society. These courageous movements did not happen overnight—it took a great amount of commitment and support from one another.

Esther went through a multi-day process to build up the courage to speak up. She asked for her community's help through fasting and prayer and she bided her time until the right moment came up to ask the question. It causes us to ponder: how can we give ourselves the same luxury when trying to make hard decisions? Do we go to our communities for support? Do we give ourselves time to figure out the best way forward? Do we remember our values, and what's at stake?

Esther's story is compelling because of how much "divine chance" is embedded in the narrative. She just happened to become a queen, who heard about a plot to kill her people, and had enough favor with the king to do something about it. In the midst of seemingly random occurrences, God was at work behind the scenes, setting up liberation.

As we ponder on our lives today, there is a possibility that beneath the surface, God is setting us up for something great. The question is: do we have eyes to see it?

Spirit Matters
MICHELLE RADFORD, 2021   OIL ON CANVAS

Reflect

PAUSE

Sit up straight.

Take a deep breath.

Using the art element (on the previous page),
take a moment to reflect on the story.

PONDER

Invite God to speak to you:

I.

Where do you hope God is working behind the
scenes in your life?

II.

Are there any circumstances in your life that you're
scared of and need courage?

III.

How can you connect to community around you in
difficult circumstances?

IV.

Where do you have a platform to speak up for others in your life?

PRAY

God who works
behind the scenes,
grant me the courage of Esther.
Give me eyes to see
where I can join in
with the love of God
for all people.
Amen.

Hagar

The Story of Hagar

SYNOPSIS

A pregnant Hagar flees amidst threat to her and her child's existence; while in the wilderness, an angel sees her, and shares God's vision for her future.

KEY MOMENT:	FULL READINGS:
Genesis 16	Genesis 16, 21:8-21

Read

Hagar's story begins wrapped up between Abram and Sarai. God has promised to make Abram and Sarai into a great nation with many descendants. But a decade has passed and still they find themselves bearing no children. In an act of desperation and dismissal of God's promise, Sarai decides to take matters into her own hands. She exercises authority over her maidservant, Hagar, to serve as a surrogate mother—giving her to her husband, Abram, in hopes to have descendants through Hagar.[1]

Soon, Hagar becomes pregnant and Sarai—out of jealousy and anger—despises Hagar and mistreats her. Hagar finds herself in a subservient position, alone as an enslaved woman. But in an act of her own agency, Hagar flees into the wilderness.[2]

There the angel of the Lord earnestly seeks Hagar. The angel asks questions with great compassion and care as the angel lets Hagar tell her own story.

"Where have you come from and where are you going?"[3]

The questions spur Hagar and invite her to search for identity, belonging, and acknowledgment of her lived reality. Of course the angel already knows the answer to them! Yet the angel gives Hagar a voice and an opportunity to feel seen.

"I am running away..."[4]

SEEING OTHERS / VALUE

What is an enslaved, pregnant woman to do in the desert with no provision, no possessions and no covering in a patriarchal, enslaving society? She finds herself in the desert of her own despair. But the angel comforts her, values her, and gives her vision for her future.

The angel says she will have descendants that are too many to count. And she will have a son named *Ishmael*—whose name means "God hears".[5] The angel sees Hagar's difficult situation but declares a new story for her. In an act of gratitude and praise, Hagar responds to her son's naming with God's naming. She raises her voice back and is the first recorded person—and woman—to name God: *El Roi*, which means, "You are the God who sees me."[6] She becomes a mother of the faith for all those who have had to leave home because home was not safe. All who had to leave their country because their country was not safe. She sees God, and God sees her.

We find a lot of "firsts" in the story of Hagar. We have the first recorded revelation of an angel of the Lord. We see the first time the angel performs an "ultrasound" in Scripture. We see the first time an angel names a child while it is still in the mother's womb.

Amidst her strenuous circumstance, God makes *Hagar*, whose name literally means "the foreigner", the center of the story—providing for Hagar and giving her a new future. While Sarai only saw Hagar as an instrument to make herself great, God truly sees Hagar as a wholly loved and cherished human being. It is a demonstration of what it means to see others—to find value in them as children of God.

[5] Genesis 16:11 / [6] Genesis 16:13

The story of Hagar urges us to ask questions on who we choose to value and bring to the center of our own narratives. Who is the last? The lost? The least? The lonely? The misunderstood? The mistreated? Do we see these people?

We live in a fractured moment in history—there are more refugees than anytime in history; as the wealth gap increases there are more and more people being left behind. Amidst these pains we can look to Hagar as a mother of the faith, and find comfort that God values and centers those most often forgotten. God's eyes never stop seeking and searching for those in need—and we, too, are invited to know this, and then do the same. How do we choose to value others? How do we come alongside our strangers and ask questions of compassion: *where have you come from and where are you going?*

Invite the Spirit to help you see with the Seeing One.

The Seine at Giverny

CLAUDE MONET, 1897

OIL ON CANVAS

Reflect

PAUSE

Sit up straight.

Take a deep breath.

Using the art element (on the previous page),
take a moment to reflect on the story.

PONDER

Invite God to speak to you:

I.

When was there a moment in time where you felt
unseen, then or now?

II.

How can the community of God's people embody
the name of "The God who sees"?

III.

Who are the unseen around you? How can you
make them the center of your story?

PRAY

To the God who sees me
and sees every tear I have ever shed,
thank you for never taking your eyes off of me.
Give us eyes to see the person
next to us that feels unseen.
Help us find their value.
Help us not to give into despair
or be paralyzed by injustice.
Grant us peace even as we work for peace.
Amen.

Hannah

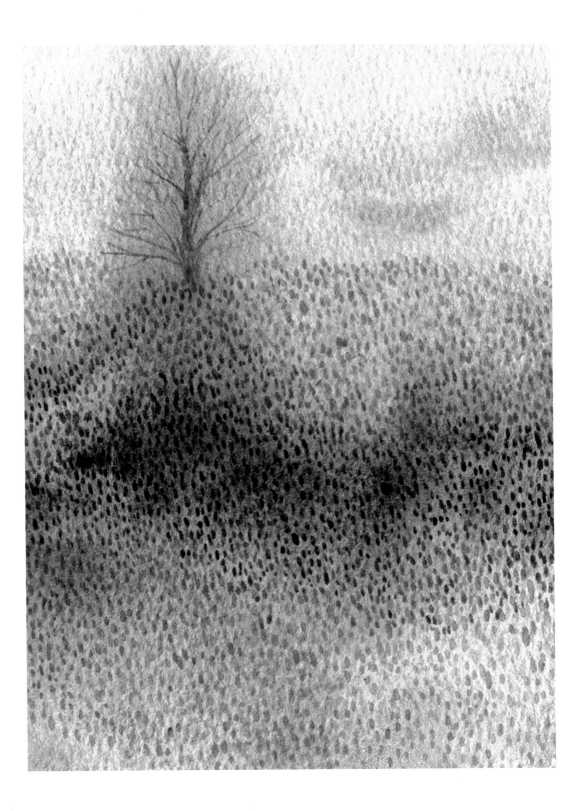

The Story of Hannah

SYNOPSIS

A childless woman, Hannah, faces an uncertain future; with hope, she offers her sorrow to God year after year and experiences transformation along the way.

KEY MOMENT:
1 Samuel 1:1-20

FULL READINGS:
1 Samuel 1:1-2:10, 18-21

Read

OUTLINE

Hannah is introduced as "a woman who is deeply troubled."[1] She was one of Elkanah's two wives, the other was named Peninnah. Hannah endured the humiliation of seeing her husband father multiple children with his other wife while she remained childless.[2] Perhaps Hannah had a deep longing to feel those first flutters that flower into tiny kicks inside her belly; perhaps she longed to give birth to a child that had her eyes and Elkanah's hands. But her pain deepened each time Peninnah attained what it seemed she could not.

Hannah's trouble may have also been driven by the social and economic consequences of being childless. In this hierarchical and patriarchal society, Hannah's gender alone made her vulnerable and placed her on the margins of society. Being unable to bear children would have been seen as yet another mark against Hannah, pushing her further to the edge of the community. Furthermore, upon the death of their husbands, women relied on their children—particularly their sons—for their protection and economic provision of their everyday needs. Who would care for Hannah in her old age if she had no children? Hannah's present standing within her community and her very future hinged on her ability to bear children. Hannah was deeply troubled indeed.

Hannah's husband, Elkanah, made some attempt to console his wife. When the household traveled to Shiloh to make their sacrifices to God, Elkanah gave Hannah "a double portion,"[3] presumably more than he gave to Peninnah and her children, to give back to the Lord. Elkanah may have wanted to show his love for Hannah though she remained without children, but Hannah could not be consoled—all she could do was weep. Even food had lost its appeal.[4] Peninnah, seeing Hannah's distress, did not respond with kindness or empathy. She chastised and humiliated Hannah, which surely only deepened Hannah's anguish. This was Hannah's life, locked in a cycle of despair.

But in the midst of her weeping, Hannah had a practice of going to the house of the Lord year after year. She was relentless. What else could Hannah do? Facing an uncertain future, she sought the only one who could hold every tear she had ever cried, but also the only one who could provide the child for whom she prayed.

During one particular trip to the temple, it seems the grief that took up residence in Hannah's heart is especially exposed, her sense of desperation particularly perceptible. She rushes past Eli, the priest who was sitting outside, tears already flowing from her eyes. In this moment, her surroundings and her appearance are unimportant. Out of the depths of her distress, "she prayed to the Lord weeping bitterly."[5]

Hannah offers up both her pain and her petition to God. She asks that God see her misery and give her the son for whom she had prayed for years. She offers the child that had not yet been conceived, back to God—the only giver of life. Her prayers are so fervent that Eli believes her to be drunk.[6] Hannah quickly corrects him. It is not wine that has been poured out, but her very soul. After baring her sorrow before God, Hannah's appetite returns and a smile finally graces her lips.[7] She rejoins her husband and they eat and drink together. Hannah's circumstances are the same: she has no child, only her tears before God. But God is beginning to transform her.

We do not know precisely how many years Hannah waits. How many times did she return to the temple, her eyes filled with tears, but her womb empty? What the text does make clear is that God answered Hannah's prayers. "In the course of time"[8], the Lord remembered Hannah and she gave birth to a son named Samuel. Hannah's weeping turned to joy as she prayed, "There is no Holy One like the Lord, there is no one besides you; there is no Rock like our God."[9]

[4] 1 Samuel 1:7 / [5] 1 Samuel 1:10 NIV / [6] 1 Samuel 1:14 / [7] 1 Samuel 1:18 / [8] 1 Samuel 1:19 NIV / [9] 1 Samuel 2:2 NIV

Hannah was a woman who knew sorrow. We may not all be able to relate to the particularities of Hannah's story as an Ancient Near Eastern woman relegated to the margins of society by her gender and childlessness. However, each of us knows of pain and suffering. We, as individuals and communities, will experience grief differently, in kind, frequency, and degree. We lose loved ones to death or broken relationships. We wrestle with addiction, disease, depression, and anxiety. We suffer under the weight of injustice because of where we are born, the color of our skin, whom we love, or because we are poor. Sorrow will find us all. What, then, will we do when it comes?

Sometimes, weeping turns to singing as it did for Hannah. When that happens, it is cause for celebration and great joy. But sometimes prayers go unanswered; and like Hannah, we have only uncertainty and pain. Sorrow can be a greedy companion, demanding all of our energy, diminishing our capacity to hope, and drying up our very faith. It can seem difficult, if not impossible, for hope to spring up in the midst of sorrow.

But Hannah's story teaches us to cultivate hope even as the tears flow and our prayers go unanswered. Despite her situation, she had a practice of prayer and a posture of radical honesty before God, not just on one occasion, but year after year. We too are free to bring every ounce of our pain before God, who can hold every kind of sorrow—that of our own lives and the kind we hold in solidarity with our neighbors. When we pray, we can believe we are not shouting into the ether. Rather, we are speaking to the Creator of the Universe and the Giver of Life. God sees our anguish and knows it for himself. We don't pray only for the removal of pain. Instead, the regular and relentless practice of prayer gives voice to our deepest distresses—and through it transforms us into a people who can find joy in spite of pain.

LILIYA RODNIKOVA, 2020   WATERCOLOR

Reflect

PAUSE

Sit up straight.

Take a deep breath.

Using the art element (on the previous page),
take a moment to reflect on the story.

PONDER

Invite God to speak to you:

I.

Are there any circumstances in your life that have brought you sorrow recently?

II.

What would it look like for us as individuals and as a community to embody Hannah's practice of prayer and posture of radical honesty before God? What steps can you take toward that this week?

III.

Where do you see opportunities to listen and hold the anguish of others in your community?

PRAY

God of sorrow,
give me the relentless faith of Hannah.
Teach me to trust you
with every ounce of my sorrow,
and to hold the sorrow of others.
We long to know joy again,
as we wait for our prayers to be answered.
Amen.

Accepting Grace

Jacob & Esau

The Story of Jacob & Esau

SYNOPSIS

After stealing his brother Esau's inheritance, Jacob lives life under threat and learns what it means to accept grace from his adversaries.

KEY MOMENT:	FULL READINGS:
Genesis 33	Genesis 25:19-28:22, 32-33

Read

OUTLINE

Born to Rebekah and Isaac, Jacob was the younger twin of his brother Esau. The story of his birth gives the reader some immediate clues to the complex status he will hold in life; God tells Rebekah that the two born of her "will be separated," and that "one people will be stronger than the other, and the older will serve the younger."[1] As the twins are delivered, Jacob comes out clutching the heel of his brother Esau.[2] This birth account sets the stage for his winding tale of mistakes, trauma, wounds, and transformation.

Their saga begins as Jacob, jealous of his brother's birthright as the firstborn, sets out to steal a blessing of inheritance meant for Esau. In a moment that sounds as far-fetched as it does dramatic, Jacob tricks his aging, semi-blind father by impersonating Esau during the blessing ritual. This act of deception confers the blessing upon Jacob, by which Esau is understandably enraged.[3]

With his life under threat by Esau, Jacob flees. The estranged brothers spend many years apart, building their own families and amassing their own wealth. Jacob continues his pattern of duplicity, in desperate bid after bid to prove his own worthiness to himself and others. In doing so, he embroils himself in numerous deadly conflicts, all the while never quite escaping the cast of Esau's shadow.

The height of their conflict reaches its peak as Jacob learns that Esau is coming with four hundred men to exact revenge on him and his family.[4] Jacob splits up his wives and children and their servants, commands them stay behind, and walks out ahead to meet Esau's company. He is prepared to die at the hands of his brother.[5]

ACCEPTING GRACE

[1] Genesis 25:23 NIV / [2] Genesis 25:26 / [3] Genesis 27:14-41 / [4] Genesis 32:6 / [5] Genesis 33:1-3

But Jacob does not get what he expects. Instead of being met with violence and rage, the story says that "Esau ran to meet Jacob and embraced him; he threw his arms around his neck and kissed him. And they wept."[6] What Jacob anticipated as the end of the road, the death of the blessing, the loss of the promise, was not the final word.

Still, perhaps on account of the traumas that he carries, Jacob does not fully recognize the grace that Esau offers him. He still feels the pull of old fears and insecurities. Esau offers to travel alongside him, but Jacob responds by saying: "So let my lord go on ahead of his servant, while I move along slowly at the pace of the flocks and herds before me and according to the pace of the children."[7] Jacob is communicating something about his own fear, albeit indirectly. He is anticipating, even after Esau's embrace, that his brother will come up from behind to kill him; as if the grace is too good to be true or too farfetched to be trusted.

Jacob is wrong. Instead of rejection, it is reunion. Instead of abandonment, it is affection. Relationship is both reassured and reconciled. He has to learn how to accept grace from an unexpected source.

TODAY

God seems to pay particular attention to controversial people; and the character of Jacob is no exception. His story is marked by self-doubt, insecurity, and fraud. The choices he makes throughout his life are not parables of virtue or exemplary in any way. Yet his role in the formation of the Jewish people could not be overstated. Not long before the beginning of our passage he was renamed Israel by an angel, going on to be the father of the twelve tribes of Israel. These are the kinds of complex people that are mixed up in God's story.

[6] Genesis 33:4 / [7] Genesis 33:14

As we recall our own moments of crisis, we may discover there is a part of Jacob in all of us. Many of us know exactly what it is like to come into this world clutching the ankle of someone else's promise and someone else's blessing. Others of us have been antagonized because of who we are or what we look like. Still some of us are faced with the consequences of our own mistakes, confronted with the ways we have hurt others.

The grace of this story for our lives today is that just as Esau looks on Jacob with unexpected tenderness, the heart of God also sees something different about ourselves than we do. When we are haunted by the ghosts of our past and convinced that our traumas are eternal, God sees us with an eye for beauty. It is this grace that gives Jacob cause to exclaim to Esau, "For to see your face is like seeing the face of God [. . .] for God has been gracious to me."[8] Jacob learns to accept grace.

Like Jacob, when we have internalized the limiting belief that love is scarce and that our worst mistakes define our stories indefinitely, we have a God who gently intervenes to remind us that we are wrong. The opportunity in this story is to remember that not only is there grace available to us, but that we must also learn to accept it in all forms it may come.

Swirling Snow (Tomoe no yuki)
KAMISAKA SEKKA, 1909-1910   INK AND COLOR ON PAPER

Reflect

Sit up straight.

Take a deep breath.

Using the art element (on the previous page), take a moment to reflect on the story.

Invite God to speak to you:

I.

Where does your own story feel complicated? Are there ways in which you feel burdened by your past?

II.

Do you believe love is abundant? What prevents you from accepting grace for yourself? From others? From God?

Gracious God,
I open myself to you.
Amidst all the wrongdoings,
may I seek to know
your love is abundant.
Today and tomorrow,
may I see this world
with your eyes.
Amen.

Wisdom Amidst Successes

Jethro & Moses

The Story of Jethro & Moses

SYNOPSIS

Jethro gives to his son-in-law, Moses, practical wisdom on how to govern their newly-liberated nation amidst the burdensome challenges that come with great success.

KEY MOMENT:
Exodus 18:13-27

FULL READING:
Exodus 18

Read

OUTLINE

We pick up our story at the height of Moses' success. He has just led the nation of Israel out of slavery in Egypt. He parted the Red Sea. He watched God feed thousands with manna and produce water from a rock. He just won his first battle against the Amalakites. God has been faithful!

Chapter 18 reintroduces an unexpected character, Moses's father-in-law, Jethro. When Jethro visits he cannot help but praise the Lord for his faithfulness and blessings. When Jethro hears Moses' story and all that God has done, he recognizes the greatness of the God of Israel and offers sacrifices to the Lord. They celebrate what God has done with a sprawling feast that all the elders of Israel attend.[1]

The next day, however, Jethro is alarmed by Moses' leadership style. From dawn till dusk, Moses sits as a judge for the people. He, alone, hears all the disputes and conflicts pooled from the thousands of people that he led out of Egypt. Jethro asks why Moses is doing all this.[2]

Moses replies that the people are coming to him to hear the will of God.

Despite Moses' successes—all of which are truly praiseworthy—Jethro has deep concern for his son-in-law. "What you are doing is not good," Jethro says. "You and these people who come to you will only wear yourselves out. The work is too heavy for you; you cannot handle it alone."[3]

WISDOM AMIDST SUCCESSES

Pause for a moment and realize to whom Jethro is speaking. This is Moses, prophet of God, Egypt's plague-bringer, parter of the Red Sea. Even more, Jethro understands the deeper character development in Moses. Jethro knew that Moses fled after an Israelite slave mocked him saying, "Who made you ruler and judge over us?"[4] He knew Moses felt inadequate and inarticulate.[5] And he heard how even the Israelite leaders criticized Moses by saying, "May the Lord look on you and judge you!"[6] All of Moses' growth and struggle has finally led to him being the *respected judge* of Israel speaking the word of the Lord.

But even amidst the success of Moses' life, Jethro sees his son-in-law's limits. It would've been so easy to be a yes-man to the budding leader of a nation. Jethro, however, vigilantly seeks Moses' holistic thriving. To keep Moses from burning out, Jethro shares three pieces of wisdom.

First, he affirms Moses as the people's representative before God. Second, he encourages Moses to teach the people how to discern God's will for themselves. And third, he instructs Moses to delegate his position as a judge to other capable, God-fearing individuals.[7]

Moses implements this advice, and his workload is made manageable. Because of this simple, yet difficult conversation, Jethro forever changes the format of Israel's governance. Here we experience a picture of a community flourishing together, sharing wisdom, and living humbly before God and each other.

[4] Exodus 2:14 NIV / [5] Exodus 4:10 / [6] Exodus 5:21 / [7] Exodus 18:19-23

We are blessed to live in a time in which we have countless ways to make a better world. We have the internet which allows us to build relationships with people anywhere on the globe. We have social media that allows us to influence hundreds of people with the press of a button. We have jobs that provide helpful services to others.

These structures and systems allow us to pursue good things. Similar to Moses, however, we may mistakenly justify working past our limits if it is for a "good thing". Perhaps we may even lean on our past successes, capabilities, and triumphs as rationalization for toiling further. Jethro's invitation for Moses—and all of us—is to let go of the continual need to strive for more, to lean on others, and to be at peace with God.

Additionally, our culture teaches us that being a good supporter means telling people they *can* do more. We so often goad people on to striving for more success without thinking of our friends' well-being or caring for their souls. Everyone wants to encourage, but being a voice of discerning wisdom is more difficult. Cinema and story have told us that the sidekick always encourages their hero to be the best or the strongest or the most powerful.

This is not the model of wisdom Jethro demonstrates. Jethro knows that Moses needs others to help him as he pursues the blessings of his nation. He has Moses divest the authority and the success that has been given to him to other capable people. Jethro cares more deeply for Moses' soul than his success or power. We, too, are invited to look after others like Jethro. Do we see others beyond their external achievements? Do we speak up when we see them struggling internally? In doing so we show the very care of God.

The Valley of Mexico from
the Santa Isabel Mountain Range
JOSÉ MARÍA VELASCO, 1875   OIL ON CANVAS

Reflect

PAUSE

Sit up straight.

Take a deep breath.

Using the art element (on the previous page), take a moment to reflect on the story.

PONDER

Invite God to speak to you:

I.

What good things has God done in your life? Celebrate those.

II.

In your pursuit of more success or blessings, are there ways you are struggling, over-working, or burning out?

III.

Are there people who you trust to speak wisdom into your life? Send a message to thank them for how they have cared for you.

IV.

Are there people who trust you to speak wisdom into their lives? How have you done so?

PRAY

God of freedom,
teach me to be free from the pursuit of *more*.
I pray for humility and rest,
and the wisdom to let go of that
which I am not meant to carry.
I pray for courage,
and the words to speak life into the lives of others.
Teach me to rest in your love,
God, who has first loved me.
Amen.

John the Baptist & the Crowd

The Story of John the Baptist & the Crowd

SYNOPSIS

The prophet, John the Baptist, prepares the way for the coming Messiah and calls the crowd of people towards repentance.

KEY MOMENT:	FULL READINGS:
Luke 3:1-20	Luke 1, 3:1-22

Read

OUTLINE

Somewhere along the Jordan River, the word of God comes to a man in the wilderness—a man we know as John the Baptist. This defining moment begins a call to ministry and makes a way for God's coming kingdom.

Reverberating on the hills of the Judean wilderness, John, recalling the words of the prophet Isaiah, speaks of preparing and cultivating the soil of the people's hearts.[1] The way is to be made smooth and ready— every valley filled in, every high place made low, and every obstacle removed. His declarations are a visual metaphor for a message of equity, which calls for justice for the oppressed, commands care for the poor, and rebukes people who wrongly use their power. His invitation echoes far beyond the banks of the Jordan River, calling all to repent and be baptized.

Many hear his call and come to be baptized. However, upon seeing the crowd, John rebukes them harshly, calling them a "brood of vipers"[2]. He sees that these people are simply trying to "flee from the coming wrath"[3], and he suggests their injustices and predatory behaviors have no place in God's coming kingdom. Despite his severe rebuke, he offers them a way forward: to bear good fruit in keeping with repentance. It is a plea to change—or the ax lies at the ready to cut down every tree bearing rotten fruit.[4]

When John utters these harsh words, the people collectively reflect, "What should we do?"[5] John tells them that the path to repentance is living justly: to share their clothing and food with those who have

REPENTANCE

none, and not to extort or take advantage of other people. Speaking to a diverse crowd that includes the rich and the poor, as well as tax collectors and soldiers—John wants them to change.[6]

With these directions, John boldly declares a baptism of repentance—a baptism that isn't merely submerging into water, but an immersion into the love, justice, and tangible care for others. Responding to the crowd's murmuring of a coming Messiah, John goes further and speaks of another coming baptism by the Holy Spirit.[7] John continues to preach his baptism of repentance and the good news of a coming Messiah until he is arrested by a threatened King Herod.[8]

At its core, the story of John the Baptist is an invitation to *repent*—to change one's mind. Like John, we are invited to call others to repent. Surprisingly to many, John's call to repentance is not about accepting a set of abstract theological principles. Instead, it's about turning away from selfishness and exploitation—and locating the real needs of the most vulnerable among us. To share clothes and food with one another, and not to take advantage of or threaten others.

When we see injustice and suffering in the world, how often do we call out the perpetrator? Do we remain silent and complacent? When we remain silent, it may be out of a desire for peace. However, more often than not our silence helps the perpetrator and leaves victims feeling more alone and forgotten. Instead, John demonstrates a radical boldness to call people to the type of ethics that Jesus lives out—active peace-making, full of love and care for the least. We are called to show others these unjust realities and invite them to repentance.

[6] Luke 3:11-14 / [7] Luke 3:16 / [8] Luke 3:20

Like the crowd, we are also invited to repentance ourselves. Upon John's harsh words the crowd could have easily become defensive, rejecting John and leaving. Instead, they decide to lean in and be curious; they ask John how they can change. Their response prompts us to question what we do when others call *us* towards repentance. Are we defensive, hardened, and brash? Or are we soft, curious, and open?

Just like the crowd, this story is an open invitation to all of us to repent, seek justice, and actively care for others—and to find Jesus through it all.

Seascape; Sunset

MARTIN JOHNSON HEADE, 1861   OIL ON CANVAS

Reflect

PAUSE

Sit up straight.

Take a deep breath.

Using the art element (on the previous page),
take a moment to reflect on the story.

PONDER

Invite God to speak to you:

I.

How often do we hear the call to repent? How do
we receive that call? How do we give that call? What
does real repentance look like?

II.

How do our lives reflect the coming Kingdom that
John the Baptist was preaching? Can we repent for
the ways in which they do not?

PRAY

God of the Coming Kingdom,
may we hear your prophetic words
and turn towards the call
to repentance.
May we be baptized and live justly,
making the way for your Way.
Amen.

Loyalty / Chosen Family

Jonathan

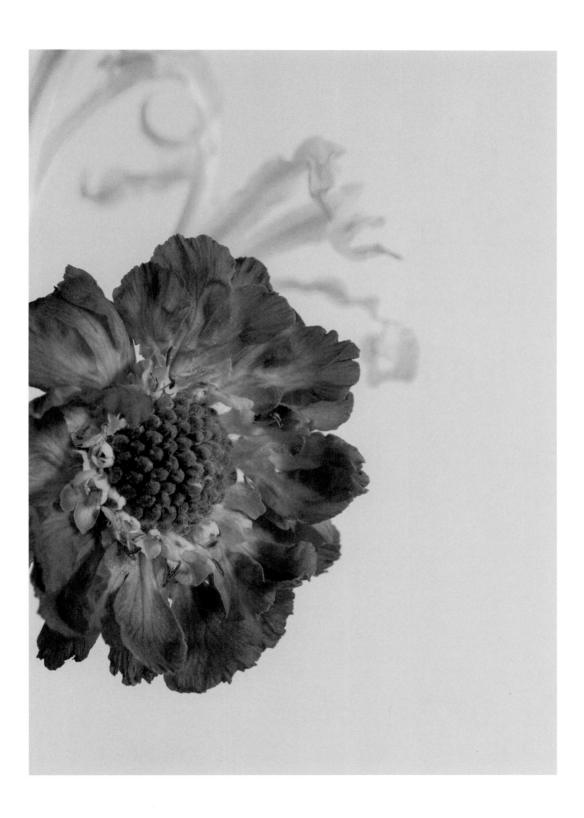

The Story of Jonathan

SYNOPSIS

When Jonathan finds himself in a broken family, he seeks the love and loyalty he deserves in David, and the two face challenges as chosen family.

KEY MOMENT:
1 Samuel 20

FULL READINGS:
1 Samuel 18-21, 2 Samuel 9

Read

Jonathan is the eldest son of King Saul, the first king of Israel. As the first born son, he was born into the expectation of carrying on his father's legacy, but his relationship with his father was rocky. Instead, he found a loyal companion in David, a man who was secretly anointed to be king of Israel after God rejected Saul as king in God's eyes.[1] David and Jonathan made a covenant—pledging their love and loyalty to each other.[2] Jonathan, the one expected to become king after Saul's death, instead pledges his loyalty to the newly anointed king, even though Saul continued to sit on the throne.

Jonathan finds himself in a complicated relationship with two men who both believe they have a claim to the throne. The one Jonathan is related to by blood is brash, angry, and insecure. The one Jonathan is related to by covenant is considered successful, strong, and gentle. It would have been hard managing these complex relationships in any scenario, but so much more difficult once Saul determined he wanted to kill David.

After an attack on his life,[3] David seeks out Jonathan for support and intel as to why Saul wants him dead. Jonathan can't imagine that his father would want to kill David. Though their relationship is rocky, surely Jonathan would have heard about this plot from his father![4] But David, recalling the recent attempt on his life, guesses Saul knows about their relationship and is intentionally keeping Jonathan in the dark about his plot.[5]

Together, they devise a plan for Jonathan to test Saul's feelings about David. When Jonathan informs Saul that David wouldn't be attending the New Moon festival, Saul flies into a rage, insulting Jona-

[1] 1 Samuel 16:13 / [2] 1 Samuel 18:1-4 / [3] 1 Samuel 19:15-16 / [4] 1 Samuel 20:2 / [5] 1 Samuel 20:3 **121**

than, telling him that he knows that Jonathan would rather David be king than himself, and sharing his intent to kill David. When Jonathan speaks up on David's behalf, Saul hurls a spear at Jonathan, his first born son, in an attempt to kill him.[6]

Crushed by the realization that his own father intends to kill his closest companion, Jonathan returns to the place he and David set aside to meet when the plan had been completed. Knowing the only way to save David's life was for him to flee, they tearfully say their goodbyes;[7] it's the last time they ever see each other. Before he goes, Jonathan reaffirms the covenant of loyalty they made before the Lord that bound them and their children together forever.[8]

Years later, Jonathan is killed in battle and David finally assumes the throne. Searching for any remaining family of Jonathan's that he can extend kindness to, he discovers that Jonathan's son Mephibosheth is still alive, and out of his loyalty to Jonathan, he gives Mephibosheth Saul's former property and regularly includes him at the king's table.[9]

TODAY

Jonathan's story is a story of selflessness, loyalty, and love. It brings up the question—who is our family? People we're related to by blood? Our friends? What makes a family?

Many of us grew up in families that we bonded with and trusted. They cared for us when we were in need and were there for us throughout the twists and turns of life. However, many of us didn't quite have that experience. Maybe we didn't fit in with our families or had a different context growing up. For many of us who grew up without close family ties or safety

[6] 1 Samuel 20:33 / [7] 1 Samuel 20:41 / [8] 1 Samuel 20:42 / [9] 2 Samuel 9

at home, we had to find other people to be in our corner—whether it be friends, acquaintances, classmates, congregants, or coworkers. No matter who we are or where we come from, we all deserve the unconditional love of a family.

Jonathan's blood family wasn't a safe place for him. He repeatedly fell out of favor with his dad and didn't believe his family had the right to kingship in Israel. But in the midst of his circumstances, he found David—a covenantal companion. They cared for each other, helped each other, and supported each other through incredibly difficult circumstances the way family should. They became each other's chosen family in tumultuous times.

For all of us, our close circle will likely change over our lifetimes. Old relationships might become strained, new relationships will become important, and our circumstances will change all the time. What's important is to look for the people who offer the kind of loyalty that David and Jonathan had with each other—the kind of people who have our backs through hard and good times, that will stand up for us as much as they will comfort us. Incredible things are possible when we rely on the people who have our best interests at heart.

We too can find people who are selfless, loyal, and loving. We too can embody those traits and values as we intentionally build our relationships. For some of us, our family by birth will always be our rock. But the story of Jonathan is a story that legitimizes all of the chosen family that we've built over our lifetimes. *All* of our relationships are a gift from God—and maybe the closest and most important relationships will come from the least likely places.

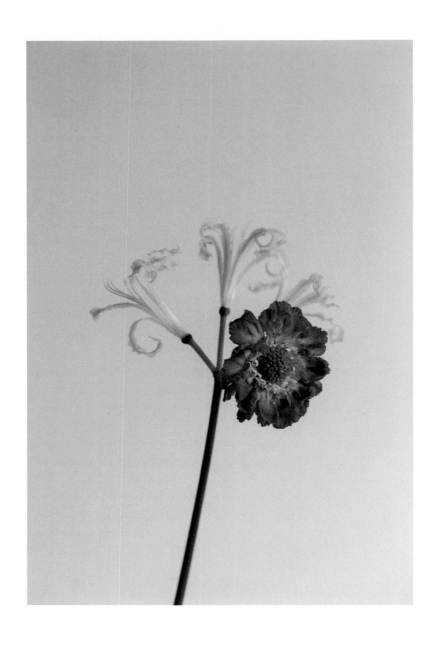

Loyalty
SAMUEL HAN, 2022　　　　　　　　　**PHOTOGRAPHY**

Reflect

PAUSE   Sit up straight.

Take a deep breath.

Using the art element (on the previous page),
take a moment to reflect on the story.

PONDER   Invite God to speak to you:

I.   What does loyalty mean to you?

II.   Who are the people in your life that you consider
family, whether you're related by birth or not?

III.   How can you nurture your relationships this week?

PRAY   God of All,
thank you for all of the people
who have been in my corner
throughout my life.
Teach me to be selfless.
Teach me to be loyal.
Teach me to love.
That I may love and be loved
by a true friend
in the same way I love myself.
Amen.

Radical Change

Josiah

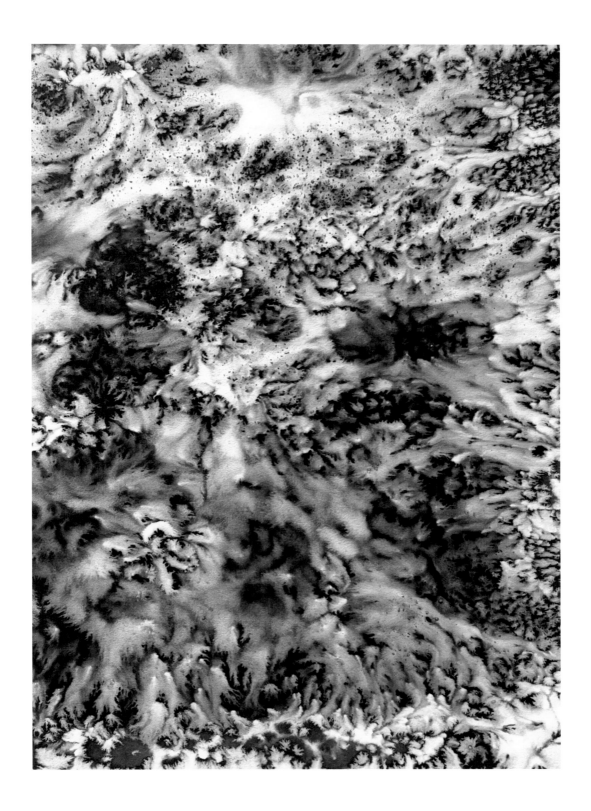

The Story of Josiah

SYNOPSIS

Josiah faces radical changes in his lifetime as king of Judah—from suddenly becoming king as a child to reorienting his kingdom as an adult. This story highlights how he responds to these changes, and how he chooses to make change happen for himself and his entire community.

KEY MOMENT:
2 Kings 22

FULL READING:
2 Kings 22-23

Read

OUTLINE

Josiah was one of the last kings of Judah before Israel's exile to Babylon. At just eight years old he was required to radically change the course of his early life by assuming the throne of his father, Amon, after Amon was assassinated by his own officials. Elected by "the people of the land"[1], Josiah was suddenly thrust into a position of power, responsibility, and legacy at an impressionable age. While 2 Kings does not offer much insight into Josiah's early childhood, something about his new life trajectory compels him to follow "the example of his ancestor David"[2] and live a life seeking God's will.

At 26 years old, eighteen years into his reign as king, Josiah begins to lean into change—rather than allowing it to be thrust upon him as he did throughout his childhood. While his forebears remained complacent, Josiah desires something different for his kingdom. First, he decides to repair the Temple.[3] He pays carpenters, builders, and masons to help begin the restoration process.

While repairing the Temple, Hilkiah the high priest and Shaphan the secretary find the Book of the Law.[4] They share it with Josiah. Upon hearing the words of the law, Josiah tears his robes, realizing his lineage has truly turned away from God![5] Immediately, yet again, the trajectory of Josiah's life is at a crossroad. This time, he wholeheartedly embraces change; he renews Judah's covenant with God[6], tears down all

RADICAL CHANGE

of the temples, shrines, and altars dedicated to false gods[7], and reestablishes Israel's generations-old observance of the Passover.[8]

Josiah changes the entire system and society of the kingdom of Judah—and it is greatly acknowledged. The Scripture reflects: "Never before had there been a king like Josiah...and there has never been a king like him since."[9]

As the old adage claims, "the only constant in life is change". We can all recount moments in our past that prompted radical change in our lives. Perhaps it is the death of a loved one, or the birth of a first child, or moving to a new home. Each of these moments shake us out of our current conformities and we are left with a choice: do we embrace the changes happening to us? Or do we try to hold on to old habits, rituals, and ways of life because they feel safe and secure?

Josiah models what a healthy dialogue with change looks like. He experiences radical moments of newness in his life—from the death of his father, to deciding to repair the temple, to discovering the Book of the Law—and in each of these moments he wholeheartedly allows, and even chooses, change. Upon assuming the throne, Josiah could have easily been like his forebears in disregarding the Temple; instead, he sees the need for a change and repairs it. Upon reading the Book of the Law, Josiah could have easily tossed it aside seeing the necessary changes it

[7] 2 Kings 23:4-20 / [8] 2 Kings 23:21 / [9] 2 Kings 23:25

prompted as too difficult to accept. Instead, Josiah immediately implements radical changes to the entire kingdom of Judah, reestablishing it as a kingdom under God.

When we are faced with change, how do we respond? The story of Josiah invites us to see change as good and necessary. It is an inevitable part of the human experience and offers opportunities, not only for a richer and fuller life, but for a more fruitful relationship with God.

Tumult
JULIA HENDRICKSON, 2022   WATERCOLOR AND SALT ON PAPER

Reflect

PAUSE

Sit up straight.

Take a deep breath.

Using the art element (on the previous page),
take a moment to reflect on the story.

PONDER

Invite God to speak to you:

I.

When has the shape of your life been altered by
radical change? How did you respond—with openness or resistance?

II.

In what areas do you need to break cycles and
choose change, even when it's hard? Where can
you choose change for the betterment of the world
around you?

PRAY

O Sovereign God,
you alone see our entire need.
When my patterns are set
and change comes my way,
grant me the courage
to respond with zeal,
to live with life anew,
in the light of your words.
Amen.

Lazarus, Martha, & Mary

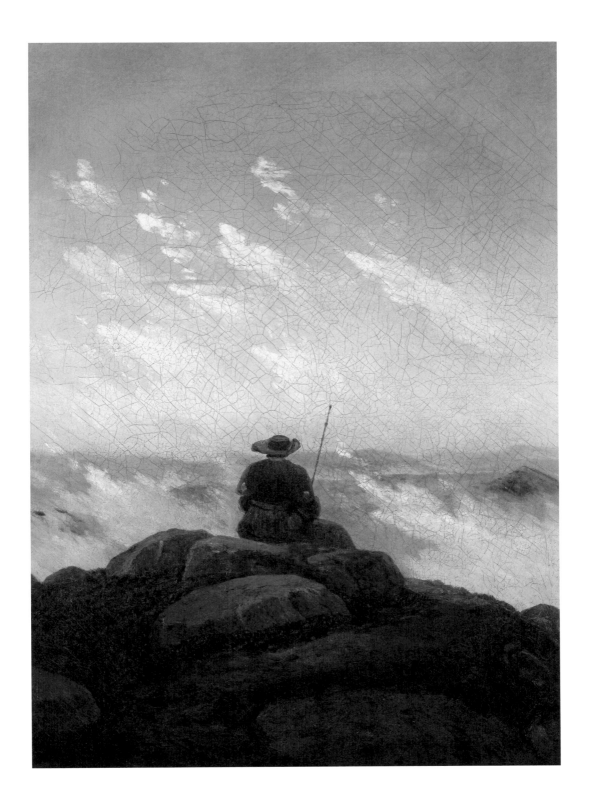

The Story of Lazarus, Martha, & Mary

SYNOPSIS

Martha and Mary navigate the delicate balance of hope and grief as they lose their beloved brother, Lazarus.

KEY MOMENT:
John 11:1-44

FULL READING:
John 11

Read

OUTLINE

Lazarus and his sisters, Martha and Mary, were from Bethany. The family hosted Jesus in their home during his ministry travels, and they were loved by Jesus. One day, Lazarus falls ill and as he begins to deteriorate, the concerned sisters send word to Jesus about their brother's condition.[1] They have seen Jesus' miraculous ability to heal and they hope he can do the same for their brother. All of them anxiously wait for Jesus to arrive.

As Lazarus becomes more and more ill, his sisters move from anticipating healing to dreading unimaginable loss. The family is soon struck with tragedy—Lazarus dies.[2] All hope dissipates. What could have been a celebration of his healing becomes a burial for his death as others gather to mourn with the family.

Once Jesus arrives, it's two days too late. Grief has rooted in place as Martha says to Jesus that *if* he had been there earlier, then their beloved brother would not have died.[3] The cloud of grief casts a shadow on any hope she had of seeing her brother again. She cannot see the promise that stands before her in Jesus—the promise for more than just life after death, but life *here and now*. She does not fully understand what Jesus means to do, but even in her grief she chooses to confide in Jesus. Meanwhile, Mary falls at the feet of her Teacher, her Rabbi, as she is anguished over the loss of Lazarus.[4] Both sisters seek the comfort of Jesus in their time of immense sadness, and all of them weep for the life lost of their brother whom they so loved.

GRIEF / HOPE

But then Jesus does something which not only pushes the boundaries of belief, but restores the ability fully to hope.

As they approach the tomb, Jesus asks them to remove the stone at the entrance. Martha, with her faith faltering in the midst of grief, tries to stop Jesus by warning him of the odor—Lazarus had already been dead four days![5] Jesus responds, reminding her that she can experience the glory of God if she holds on to her hope and belief. So they roll away the stone.

Jesus looks up and gives glory to God reminding these sisters and the community surrounding them that what is about to happen belongs to God. Jesus loudly says to Lazarus, lying lifeless in a tomb, "Lazarus, come out!"[6] He walks out of the tomb. The grief of Lazarus' family transforms into wonder. Those who witnessed the miracle put their faith in Jesus—they experience the glory of God.

Lazarus' miracle is not about just one person. It includes the story of the people around him and, ultimately, the story of who Jesus is. We see a family concerned, desperate but hopeful for the miraculous healing they know Jesus can bring. But suddenly, their hope turns to grief after their brother dies. Looking deeper, there is a bittersweet reminder of the intersection of grief and hope.

When we are suddenly met with grief it can consume us with every breath we take. We are left vulnerable and unable to see the light of tomorrow, as the people, the way of life, and the things we wished for suddenly disappear. Financial instability, aging parents, career loss, infertility, political instability, cancer or long-term illness are all forms of grief we can face today. These experiences may bring about a deep sorrow—and even a loss of hope.

Yet even in heartache we can be like Martha and Mary, and confide in Jesus. Just like them, we may not understand it fully at the moment, but we know we can trust Jesus and his promise of life. Even amidst grief, we can allow the faint cracks of hope in Jesus to seep through as we remember he is our ultimate healer.

And, so, the story ends with hope fully restored. Jesus makes death powerless, offering new life, here and now, to Lazarus. Even if it does not take the form of raising a physical body from the dead, we are all in need of this *life*: the vitality and vividness that makes existing in the world *worth it*. That is what Jesus offers, that is what he continually asks us to hope for no matter the grief and suffering and sorrow around us. In a grievous world, do we believe that there is life to be lived on the other side of grief? Can we hope for it?

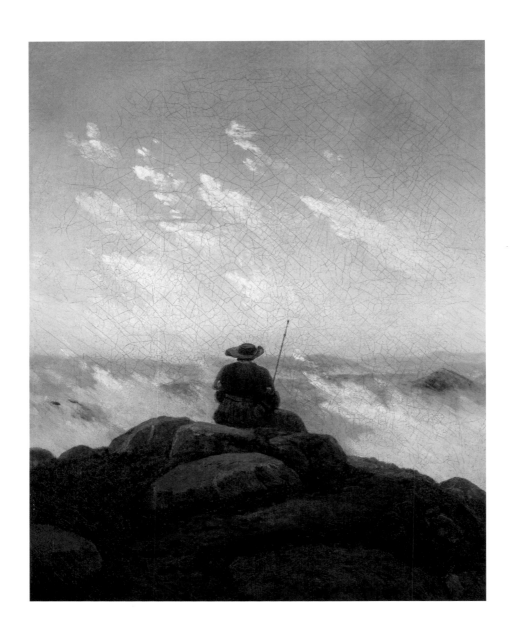

Wanderer on the Mountaintop
CARL GUSTAV CARUS, 1818

OIL ON CANVAS

Reflect

PAUSE

Sit up straight.

Take a deep breath.

Using the art element (on the previous page),
take a moment to reflect on the story.

PONDER

Invite God to speak to you:

I.

Have there been times in your life when you have
felt consumed by grief, unable to walk through it?
What does immovable grief look like?

II.

Where can you engage Jesus with honesty over these
moments of grief? How can you experience greater
hope in Jesus amidst this grief?

PRAY

God of Compassion
I am fragile and in need.
When I am consumed by grief
and sorrow overcomes my heart,
walk me from the darkness of death
to the vividness of life.
And may all my hope be found in you.
Amen.

Hospitality

Lydia

The Story of Lydia

SYNOPSIS

Lydia, a godly Greek woman of influence, participates in the Gospel message and extends hospitality to Paul and his companions on their journey.

KEY MOMENT:
Acts 16:11-15

FULL READING:
Acts 16

Read

OUTLINE

Lydia enjoys her regular trips to the riverbank, where a handful of Jews gather to pray. Her work in trading purple cloth keeps her plenty busy, successful, and wealthy; but this is one of the places where she can find kindred hearts who seek God.

Today, however, the place of prayer is extra busy. There seems to be some new people, and a man she has never seen before is teaching. The speaker introduces himself as Paul. He and his company are traveling from city to city teaching about the Messiah, and God had told them to come here to Macedonia.[1]

Paul continues to speak about Jesus Christ, this unexpected servant-king who fulfills all the prophecies of old and embraces everyone. Lydia hangs on every word. If this good news is true, then it changes everything. The Kingdom of God that Jesus spoke of means that she, this gentile woman and business owner out in Philippi, is someone *beloved* by God. She is part of God's home.

As the leader of her household, Lydia knows she must bring her family and her servants to learn about this Jesus. That very day, she and her whole household are baptized in the river.[2]

[1] Acts 16:9 / [2] Acts 16:15   **145**

But Lydia wants something even more—not just to receive the good news, but to participate in it. The good news of the Kingdom of God coming near is more than just a message; it is a welcoming hospitality that invites us to see everyone as part of our household.

Using her resources as a dealer in purple cloth, she offers to host Paul and his company for as long as they like.[3] Being associated with a traveling preacher like Paul is sure to reflect on her social standing and clientele. But she can't help it—she is changed by the good news.

God's good news is one of *hospitality*—it is a warm embrace extended to *everyone*; even those with unique intersectional identities. Lydia is one of these individuals; she is a gentile, a worshiper of God, a business owner, a woman, a head of the household, and a wealthy person. This amalgamation of identities is uncommon in the first century CE. But the good news welcomes her as it does to all.

What do we do when we're met with such a powerful, hospitable force? We welcome others into it! Lydia first shows hospitality to the rest of her household; she does not hold this good news to herself but invites them all to experience it. And then she goes further; she understands this good news of hospitality means her household, her family, has grown—Paul and his companions are now part of that household as well. She uses her unique identity and resources and warmly welcomes them into her home.

[3] Acts 16:15

Hospitality is at the core of the Gospel message. It is an enclosing air that enwraps us with all good things: love, belonging, coziness, kindness, and affection. The natural response to this experience, like Lydia, is to bring about hospitality ourselves—to share generously no matter how big or small, to invite others into our home, and to use our unique identities to show our distinctive form of neighborliness. Who can we welcome today?

Flower Baskets And Flower Pots In A Garden
ALFRED PETIT, 1887   OIL ON CANVAS

Reflect

PAUSE

Sit up straight.

Take a deep breath.

Using the art element (on the previous page),
take a moment to reflect on the story.

PONDER

Invite God to speak to you:

I.

How do you see God's good news as an expression
of hospitality?

II.

How have you experienced hospitality from others? Take a moment to express gratitude for their
generosity.

III.

Where can you uniquely share generosity and hospitality with others?

PRAY

God, thank you
for the divine example of hospitality.
Thank you for the home you have opened to me
through the Gospel message you bring.
Teach me to live with open doors
for the many siblings I have in Christ.
Amen.

Shame / Discernment

The Man Born Blind

The Story of The Man Born Blind

SHAME / DISCERNMENT

SYNOPSIS

A man born blind is miraculously healed. His healing restores his whole humanity away from shame, and towards a new found faith and belonging.

> **KEY MOMENT:**
> John 9

Read

OUTLINE

Our story opens with Jesus' disciples asking about a man who has been blind from birth. Their questioning shows a common assumption of that time period—sickness and disability are caused by sin—an assumption that this man had grown up with, hanging over his very existence.

Jesus' disciples assume that *someone* must have sinned for the man to have been born blind,[1] but who can know? Perhaps he committed some heinous act in the womb, or his parents had sinned in such a way as to be punished with a blind child. Such whispered judgments were common rhetoric as the man got older. When everyone around you assumes you or your family have earned God's punishment, shame and isolation encroach on your identity.

Undermining these assumptions, Jesus responds with a different viewpoint—the man's blindness isn't an indication of God's curse, but an opportunity for the power of God to be seen in him. How would he choose to display this?

He spits on the ground. Mixing his saliva with dirt, he creates a muddy concoction and puts it on the man's eyes.[2]

Jesus directs the man, "Go, wash yourself in the Pool of Siloam"[3], and moves along the path.

Upon washing, the man's eyes are *opened*. Who was it that realized this healing? The mud covered his ability to see the healer's face before he had left.

While the man is surely rejoicing, his neighbors, the same ones who had known him as a blind beggar, have trouble recognizing him. It could be because of his physical healing, but it's clear this man had also experienced an emotional and social healing, replacing his shame with confidence and belonging.

His transformation leads to a disagreement among the people which brings him to the Pharisees to settle the dispute. The questioning turns into an interrogation when the Pharisees realize the healing took place on the Sabbath, and the focus shifts from the healed man to the person who brought the healing.

"I think he must be a prophet,"[4] the man says.

Unhappy with the whole situation, the Pharisees bring in the man's parents as character witnesses, but their quick responses absolve themselves from the controversy surrounding their son.

The Pharisees return to questioning the man a second time. The man, frustrated by their disbelief, responds by simply stating that God only listens to those who do God's will. Only God could have the power to heal someone born blind. Perhaps the man is emboldened by his new status in society as a seeing man; however, in any case, his arguments anger the Pharisees. Enraged, they fire back with their underlying assumption: that the man's disability had been caused by his sinfulness. They throw him out of the synagogue.[5]

Hearing about the encounter, Jesus seeks out the man he healed and reveals himself as the one who had healed him. Immediately, the man puts his belief in Jesus and worships him as Lord.[6]

Jesus commends him for his discernment and ends the story with a warning to anyone who claims to see but is unable to see Jesus for who he truly is. It seems the Pharisees were the ones who were truly blind in the end.

[4] John 9:17 / [5] John 9:34 / [6] John 9:38

We can see from the Man Born Blind's story that shame and judgment are designed to keep us down and alone. As social scientist Brené Brown describes, "Shame corrodes the very part of us that believes we are capable of change". This man had grown up with the weight of the belief that his very existence was proof of God's displeasure and punishment. Not only was he navigating life with a disability, he was living as a pariah in his own town, isolated and condemned. The only option for his future was to accept pity and scorn as a beggar. We too may feel the destructive realities of shame and long to be free from its power. Shame creeps in when we feel like imposters in professional settings, or replay past rejections and mistakes in our head, or compare our lives to others whom we perceive to be more likeable.

In restoring the man's physical sight, Jesus reaches through his wall of shame, dignifies him in front of his community, and as a result, leads the man to a deeper faith which is put on display to those around him.

When our humanity is restored, it can lead to greater faith. In this story, greater faith is created in more than just a singular moment of physical healing—but rather a conscious recalibration of the man's *entire* life in light of that healing. For his whole life, such a public argument with the Pharisees would have been looked upon with disdain. Yet, as displayed by his boldness to respond publicly to his accusers, he embodies an imaginative model of faith accessible to anyone who has been marginalized through shame. It is a much needed antidote for a corroded world.

The story of the man born blind reminds us that Jesus' healing is multi-faceted; not only does Jesus heal bodies, but he heals our relationships with ourselves and the world around us. For those of us that experience shame, Jesus invites our muddy eyes to experience a renewed life.

Mammoth Hot Springs, Yellowstone
THOMAS MORAN, 1872   WATERCOLOR AND PENCIL ON PAPER

Reflect

Sit up straight.

Take a deep breath.

Using the art element (on the previous page), take a moment to reflect on the story.

PONDER

Invite God to speak to you:

I.

Are there areas in your life where you feel shame?

II.

What areas have you lost the belief you are capable of change? What would it take to grow that belief?

III.

Where have you experienced healing? In what ways are you invited to live in light of that healing?

PRAY

To the God who sees,
when shame corrodes my being,
may I be made whole by you.
Amen.

Watchfulness / Survival

Miriam

The Story of Miriam

SYNOPSIS

Miriam watches over Moses and the future of Israel, participating in the cooperative task of their survival.

KEY MOMENT:	**FULL READINGS:**
Exodus 2:1-10	Exodus 2, 15-16

Read

OUTLINE

Exodus 2 recounts the story of a group of women who thwart Pharaoh's plans and save the Hebrew child, Moses, who would go on to save the Hebrew people. A Levite couple has Moses, and seeing that the child is good, beautiful, and healthy, the mother hides the child, defying Pharaoh's order that every Hebrew boy should be killed by being thrown into the Nile.[1] Pharaoh miscalculates and thinks the Hebrew men are the threat to his rule[2], but in the end it is the women who defy him. In Exodus 1, two midwives reject Pharaoh's command to kill the Hebrew boys, and in Exodus 2 Moses' mother, sister, Pharaoh's daughter, and Pharaoh's maid refuse to obey Pharaoh and become the saviors of the Hebrew people.

When she could no longer hide Moses, his mother, Jochebed[3], creates an ark so that she can place Moses in the Nile River. Cleverly, Jochebed found a way to "obey" the word of Pharaoh, placing her son in the river, while actually disobeying Pharaoh and saving her baby. Jochebed tricks Pharaoh. Her story is an example of the trickster motif of the Ancient Near Eastern world, where those with less power find creative ways to trick the powerful. Exodus 2 views Jochebed's trickery favorably—it is even salvific!

After Moses is set on the water his sister, Miriam[4], watches Moses to see what would happen.[5] We can wonder what leads Miriam to this. Perhaps after corralling the courage to initiate the plan Jochebed can no longer watch, but Miriam cannot keep her eyes off of her brother. She takes it upon herself to become her brother's keeper, to be concerned for his life.

WATCHFULNESS / SURVIVAL

And it is fortunate that Miriam does watch. Pharaoh's own daughter sees the baby floating amidst the reeds and sends her maid to bring it. Pharaoh's daughter, knowing this is a Hebrew child and knowing her father has commanded the death of Hebrew children is still moved to have pity for the baby.[6] Miriam does not wait, she sees her moment and quickly devises a plan. Perhaps Miriam is already operating with the inspiration of God that is acknowledged when she is later named as one of the few female prophets of the Hebrew Bible. She makes herself known and speaks up to royalty, suggesting she find a Hebrew woman to nurse the baby for her. Pharaoh's daughter agrees, not knowing this means the baby will return to his own mother.[7]

This is the first time Miriam stands beside the waters to witness liberation.

Later, in Exodus 15, Miriam again stands beside the waters of the Reed Sea. The water parts for the Israelites but the Egyptians, driven by Pharaoh's violent desire to keep the Hebrew people enslaved, follow and are defeated as the waters close in on them. This Pharaoh's father had previously tried to use the life-giving waters of the Nile as a vehicle for death, but here it is as if the waters have turned back on Pharaoh himself. The people of Israel experience liberation.

At the waters edge Miriam takes a tambourine and invites all the Hebrew people to join her in a song of praise to YHWH. "Sing to YHWH"[8] is an imperative phrase. As a prophet, Miriam takes up her authority over all the people of Israel—the young, the old, and all genders. It is widely agreed that Miriam's song is one of the oldest texts of the Hebrew Bible. The Song of the Sea, sung by Moses in Exodus 15:1-18 is likely an expansion on Miriam's song. Miriam, who witnesses the birth of her brother, who watches over him, is also the prophetic witness of the birth of Israel through the waters. By the time of the New Testament, we can see Miriam's name has become revered among the Jewish people. It is even the name of Jesus' mother. English translations obscure this by translating the Greek Mariám as Mary, but she is indeed another Miriam who is called by YHWH, who witnesses the birth of a savior, and who prophetically sings God's praises at the advent of YHWH's salvation.

[6]Exodus 2:6 / [7]Exodus 2:7-10 / [8]Exodus 15:20-21

In Exodus 2 we witness the clever cooperation of the disempowered who struggle towards survival. There is much to learn here. Survival is not an individual task, but a cooperative task. It also requires that we are able to see, evaluate, and at times reject authorities that oppose well-being, even tricking the powerful to preserve life. Several commentators have noticed the story of Moses' birth is a story of internal migration and it resonates with the experiences of migrant peoples who take on extreme risk and defy political structures in order to survive.

Part of our task, like Miriam, is to remain watchful. We must look to see how it goes with our family, our neighbors, and with the vulnerable. We must remain attentive and ready. This is indeed part of Miriam's prophetic task. This watchfulness brings about the opportunity for intervention. It also brings about the opportunity to witness liberation—like the saving of baby Moses—happen all around us.

The prophetic task we are called to is also to celebrate liberation and invite others into that celebration. In Exodus 15, as Pharaoh's army is washed away by the Reed Sea, the people of Israel experience deep liberation. Miriam sees this and does not hold it to herself—she invites her people to sing! It is part of the prophetic task to see when people are set free from the variety of oppressions and enslavements they face, to not let the moment pass quietly or even with individual satisfaction, but to call everyone to praise and celebration.

IVAN OZEROV, 2019

PHOTOGRAPH

Reflect

Sit up straight.

Take a deep breath.

Using the art element (on the previous page),
take a moment to reflect on the story.

PONDER

Invite God to speak to you:

I.

How can we remain watchful on behalf of the people in our lives who are in need?

II.

How have you participated in the survival of goodness in our world?

III.

How have you celebrated with community when people are set free from oppression?

PRAY

God of Salvation,
you bring rescue to the vulnerable.
Awaken our bodies, ready our minds.
Guide our senses to watch over our neighbors,
and may we invite all to praise and celebrate
liberation in our world.
Amen.

Naaman

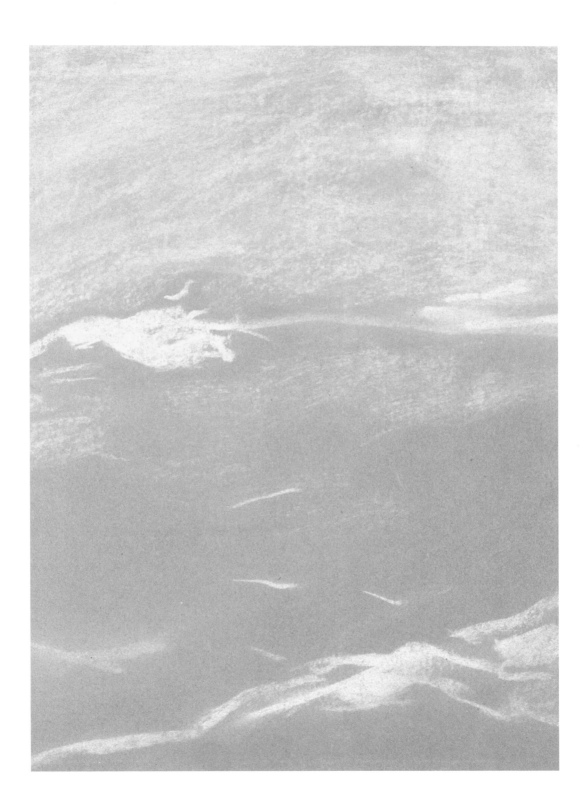

The Story of Naaman

SYNOPSIS

In an era when Aram caused great affliction to the Israelites, a military commander named Naaman is physically healed by the prophet, Elisha. Along his journey he discovers the power of openness and finds counsel from unexpected places.

KEY MOMENT:	FULL READING:
2 Kings 5:1-19	2 Kings 5

Read

OUTLINE

While the Israelites were in continual conflict with the kingdom of Aram, 2 Kings 5 accounts an unusual story of healing. Naaman was a man who held great power as a leader in the Aramean army, surrounded by respect and fear. Yet, he was plagued with a skin disease that would have caused him both physical and social distress.

It is in this context that Naaman hears from a young Israelite servant about a person who could heal him: the Israelite prophet Elisha.[1] Naaman could have easily disregarded this information. Firstly, the information is coming from a captured servant—a source not likely to be taken seriously because of their low place in society. And secondly, the information is coming from an Israelite—with whom the Arameans have intense conflict.

Despite this, Naaman, out of desperation, chooses to be open to the possibility of healing. He goes to the King of Aram to ask for permission to leave for Israel and find Elisha.

A letter travels ahead of Naaman to the King of Israel as a means of peace. Upon receiving the letter, the King of Israel is distraught, mistaking Naaman's travel as potentially hostile.[2] The prophet Elisha hears of the king's distress. Elisha sends the King of Israel a message to have Naaman sent to his home to be healed and experience God's power.

But as Naaman arrives he is not greeted by Elisha, but by Elisha's servant, Gehazi. The servant Gehazi gives Naaman instructions to wash in the Jordan River seven times to receive complete healing and restoration.[3]

On hearing this, Naaman becomes frustrated at the difference between his expectations and Elisha's methods. Why had Naaman not received more respect and been greeted by the prophet himself rather than this servant? Couldn't Elisha simply have waved his hand and called the name of God to give Naaman immediate healing? What was the difference between bathing in the Jordan River and the rivers back in Syria?

Naaman's servants, listening to his confusion and anger, remind him: wouldn't complete healing be worth seven dips in the Jordan river as preposterous as it seemed?[4] Naaman, in his rage, seems poised to ignore Elisha's instructions—but again, in his desperation, he chooses to be open to the possibility of healing. Naaman, emotionally raw and hopeful, goes down to the Jordan and follows the instructions of God's prophet. After the seventh bath, Naaman's skin is completely healed; he is finally cleansed.[5]

Amazed, Naaman returns to Elisha's house to offer gratitude for his healing, proclaiming that there is no god other than the God of Israel. Elisha sends Naaman off with a blessing of peace.

Naaman was a powerful military leader who was more likely to be in a position commanding and ordering others than listening to them. He could have easily ignored the suggestions of the Israelite servant girl, Gehazi, or his own servants, but instead—out of openness and desperation—Naaman chooses hope and listens to them. And as a result, he is healed.

When we look at our culture today we are pressed to ask if we possess the same level of openness that Naaman had. How often do we change our minds? How often are we open to other people, especially people with less social status than us? Do we believe that God is in those people? Do we believe healing can come from unexpected places?

Our culture entices us only to listen to those that are powerful, noteworthy, and familiar. But the story of Naaman reminds us that God's counsel and instructions can often come from those that society would deem lacking a voice worth listening to.

Like Naaman, we are not perfect; when we are offered something different from our expectations we may easily become frustrated or close-minded. But the invitation from Naaman is to let go of rigid expectations and be available towards the possibility of something new—even healing. Are we open and attentive?

Seagull and Waves

WINSLOW HOMER, 1884   CHALK ON BLUE BLOTTING PAPER

Reflect

Sit up straight.

Take a deep breath.

Using the art element (on the previous page),
take a moment to reflect on the story.

Invite God to speak to you:

I.

Are there areas in your life that require healing?

II.

Who do you go to in times of need? Is there an opportunity to expand your community and listen to counsel from unexpected places?

III.

How open-minded are you when you are presented with something different from your expectations?

God who heals,
teach me to find counsel
in unexpected places.
Help me be open
to new possibilities,
to new ways of living,
to new healing.
Amen.

Naomi

The Story of Naomi

SYNOPSIS

The story of Naomi is about loss, what it looks like to pick up the pieces amidst grief, and how to invite community into our experience through it all.

KEY MOMENT:	FULL READING:
Ruth 1	Ruth 1-4

Read

OUTLINE

As the Book of Ruth opens, Naomi loses her homeland. There is a famine in Bethlehem of Judah, and so Naomi, her husband, and their two sons, leave the land they have always known and settle in Moab.

There her husband dies, leaving Naomi with her two sons in a foreign land. As they settle there, each son marries a local woman. Ten years later, the unthinkable happens and both Naomi's sons die.[1] A parent losing a child is a uniquely deep grief, and Naomi experiences it twofold.

Naomi is without a homeland, without a husband, and now without any children. Her life is gutted by loss.

But her loss doesn't happen in a vacuum. Naomi has two daughters-in-law, Orpah and Ruth. And they hear some good news—that God has blessed Naomi's homeland with good crops once again, so she and her daughters-in-law can begin to make their way there.

Except.

Realizing these young women still have many years where they might raise children with new husbands, Naomi implores them to go back to Moab to their families, their gods, and their way of life. They have lost their husbands, yet their story is not over. Naomi, on the other hand, feels her age. She will have no more children. She feels the heaviness of all the loss she has endured over the years, one after another, and through it all senses God's fist raised against her. This is not simply a series of painful life events; for Naomi it holds deep spiritual significance. It shows

[1] Ruth 1:1-5

that her God is not protecting her. She knows that God holds the world, and her world has fallen apart. She feels God is against her.[2]

They weep together, and Orpah returns to her family.

But not Ruth. Ruth refuses to leave.

No matter how much Naomi pleads with her, Ruth remains. This decision means significant losses for Ruth—her homeland, her family, her gods. But while Naomi's losses were out of her control, Ruth chooses these losses. For Ruth, not remaining with Naomi would be the bigger loss. She commits to making Naomi's land, people, and God her own, and they journey toward Bethlehem together.[3]

When Naomi returns to her homeland, the people she had left so many years before welcome her back. But she needs them to know she's changed. *Naomi* means "pleasant." And she is not the Naomi they knew years ago, with a loving husband, two healthy sons, and a sense of God's benevolence toward her. Instead, she is bitter, empty, and has endured great suffering; and she needs her kindred to understand this. So she insists they call her by a new name, *Mara* "bitterness", so they will all have to acknowledge, every time they speak of her, the deep loss that God has brought into her life.[4]

As we think about the losses we have experienced, we may notice how our losses felt different depending on whether it was something we chose, or something thrust upon us.

Loss like deciding to end a relationship, moving to a new city, changing jobs—these are losses akin to Ruth. Though they contain the pain of loss, we also have a sense of choice and control. But other kinds of loss like a difficult medical diagnosis, the death of a loved one, or being let go from a job—these are losses similarly experienced by Naomi. These losses shatter us to our core precisely because they are uncontrollable, turbulent, and confusing.

In seasons where losses feel thrust upon us, like Naomi we might experience God as being against us, sending tragedies into our lives. Naomi doesn't feel the need to rescue God's reputation or qualify her experience of God with "right theology"—instead she is honest and unflinching about her spiritual life after a series of shattering losses. Do we feel such freedom when we are feeling far from God—why or why not?

Naomi even gives herself a new name, calling her community to see her and acknowledge her pain. She thereby invites us to wonder, how seriously do we take our places of pain and loss? Do we invite the people around us to see us in our pain, and to hold it with us? What name do we ask people to call us?

"From Earth's Womb:
Sand and Stone Are Earth's Memory"
DEA JENKINS, 2020

WATERCOLOR,
NATURAL PIGMENT,
PAPER, ACRYLIC MEDIUM

Reflect

PAUSE

Sit up straight.

Take a deep breath.

Using the art element (on the previous page), take a moment to reflect on the story.

PONDER

Invite God to speak to you:

I.

In what areas of your life do you want to express with more honesty (whether with God, yourself, or others)?

II.

Are there situations of pain in your own story you haven't yet acknowledged? What would it look like to grieve these situations and invite community to support you?

PRAY

God of Comfort and Sovereignty,
when I set out whole
and am brought back empty with loss,
lend me courage to be honest within.
In grief, may I turn to my heart to you
and my community,
and return help to loved ones in pain,
where wholeness is found.
Amen.

Nehemiah

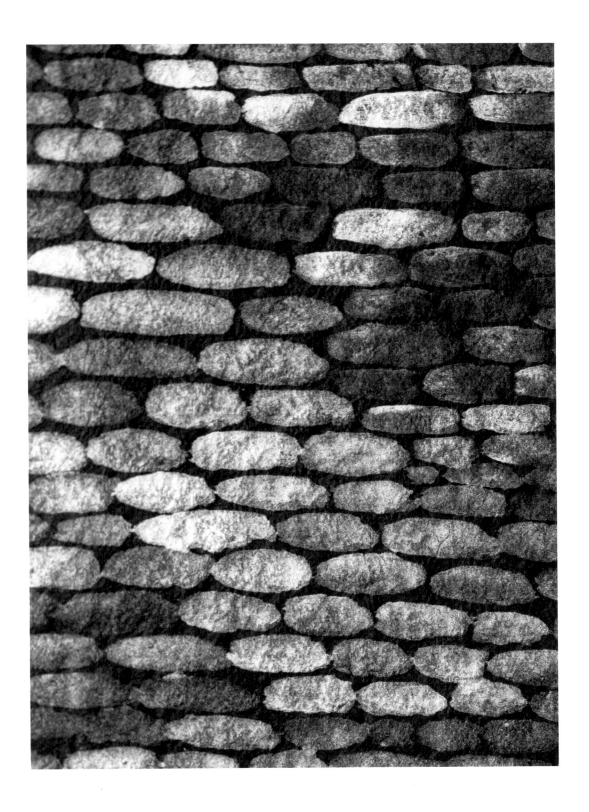

The Story of Nehemiah

SYNOPSIS

Nehemiah journeys from his place in King Artaxerxes' court to his broken homeland, awaiting God's timing with wisdom, faith, and slowness. God makes a way for Nehemiah's participation and for restoration.

KEY MOMENT:
Nehemiah 1-2

FULL READINGS:
Nehemiah 1-6, 12:27-13:31

Read

Born in Persia to parents exiled from Jerusalem, Nehemiah ascended to a place of prominence in King Artaxerxes' court as his cup-bearer.[1] In this position Nehemiah was highly trusted and would make sure the king and his guests had ample (unpoisoned) wine throughout their gatherings.

Nehemiah receives news that in Jerusalem, the homeland of his parents, the city's walls have been torn down and its gates burned. Jerusalem's strong walls are what enabled it to thrive, and for its people to flourish and dwell in greater safety. It is now in ruins. Nehemiah is devastated.[2]

For many days he slows down and takes intentional time to hold this news in his own heart and before God. Mourning, fasting, and praying, Nehemiah beseeches God to look with favor on the people of Judah and begins to wonder whether his relationship with the king might open a way for Nehemiah himself to intervene.

Still grieving the brokenness of Jerusalem, when Nehemiah comes to serve the king that spring, he cannot hide his sorrow. King Artaxerxes notices and asks about it.

Nehemiah laments that the land where his ancestors are buried is in shambles.

The king asks what he can do to help.[3]

Recognizing God's movement in this moment, Nehemiah knows this is not a time for timidity. He prays for God to work through this conversation and tells the king that he wants to travel to Judah himself to rebuild the city.

This is no small trip. Jerusalem is more than 1,000 miles from Persia, and Nehemiah knows he'll need protection as he travels, and supplies to rebuild the city's walls when he arrives. With boldness, he asks for what he needs for the repair work that is on his heart to do. The king grants all of Nehemiah's requests, which Nehemiah knows is due to God's loving intervention.

After a long journey, Nehemiah arrives in Jerusalem.

Just as Nehemiah had a time of slow inwardness with God before creating a plan to share with the king, Nehemiah again slows down and proceeds with deliberate, prayerful intentionality. Initially he holds his plans to rebuild the wall only within his own heart. With a small group of men, he surveys the tragic ruins of the city and takes time to let his plans and feelings percolate.[4]

Finally, he tells the city officials and religious leaders what he has come to Jerusalem to do.

As he tells the Jewish leaders of his plan, he relies not merely on his own passion and charisma to persuade them, but emphasizes that God has provided for him and opened the way for this to happen all along the way. They joyfully welcome his plan.[5]

Some city officials mock him scornfully, but Nehemiah remains steadfast in the face of their derision, reiterating his plans to rebuild the wall, knowing that "The God of heaven will help us succeed."[6]

TODAY

When we are grieved by a situation of brokenness, how quickly do we respond? And how much do we trust God to make a way for restoration?

[4] Nehemiah 2:16 / [5] Nehemiah 2:18 / [6] Nehemiah 2:19-20

We might notice something that needs healing on a grand scale, like Nehemiah's project for the welfare of a whole city. Alternatively, it might be on a smaller scale like bringing a new form of care and justice into our neighborhood, or for God's healing to enter a longstanding dynamic in our family, or for something that needs repair in our own heart.

Nehemiah's deliberate and prayerful slowness invites us to reflect on our own pace of engaging with God about the places in need of repair around and within us—no matter how daunting. And it reminds us that God is the one who will make a way.

We may feel overwhelmed when we notice that something is broken; we may find it difficult to respond or act at all. On the other hand, in a hurried society, we might respond with immediate action to gain a sense of false control over the situation.

Nehemiah shows us another way. He does act (which is crucial!), but it's surrounded in prayer, slowness, and intentionality. Each step along the way includes him paying attention—to his own feelings, to his surroundings, and maybe most importantly, to how God is showing up. His slowness is enabled by his persistent trust in God, and God responds in partnership with Nehemiah. What seemed like an overwhelming task is possible because God is forging a path forward.

What would it look like to respond to the brokenness we notice in our lives and our world with the deliberate slowness and persistent trust that Nehemiah has? Could we also ground ourselves in prayer, make space for feelings of pain and grief, and remain attentive to God's power and movement? Could we trust God to work with us towards restoration?

Static

ERIC TAI, 2021   SILVER ON PAPER

Reflect

Sit up straight.

Take a deep breath.

Using the art element (on the previous page), take a moment to reflect on the story.

PONDER

Invite God to speak to you:

I.

What was a time when you rushed in to fix a problem without spending time with yourself and with God first? What might you have done differently if you had brought the issue to God before acting?

II.

Do you have a story in which God made even the most unlikely or surprisingly practical aspects come into place for goodness to be done?

III.

How can we be more sensitive to when God is doing more than we know, so that we can attentively wait for our time to participate in restoration?

PRAY

O God of restoration,
may I see your way being made
behind the scenes
and in the unexpected things.
May I know when to be slow
and allow you to set me up
to participate in making the world whole.
Amen.

Onesimus

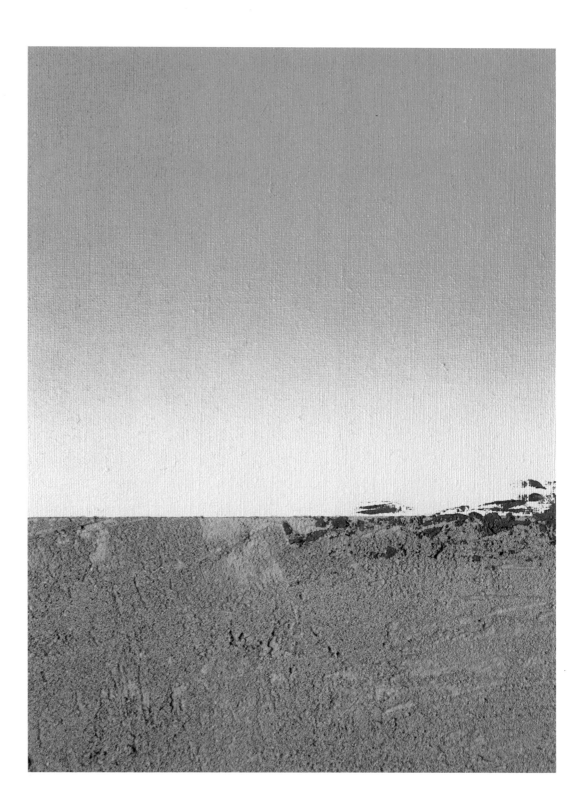

The Story of Onesimus

SYNOPSIS

In this chapter, we contemplate how the Gospel story could stir Onesimus to chase freedom from slavery in the face of institutionalized oppressive power.

KEY MOMENT:
Philemon 1

Read

The story of Onesimus' journey to freedom is laid out in an advocacy letter from Paul to Onesimus' former master, Philemon. Onesimus was Philemon's slave—until he freed himself and escaped the bonds of slavery. Paul writes on his behalf, vouching for Onesimus to be received by Philemon with peace, not as a slave once again, but as a free man who would be considered an equal.[1] Issues of power, honor, dignity and agency are all on the table with the *good news* of Christ and the *Kingdom of God* spreading throughout the Mediterranean. The Roman-ruled society of the time rests on the idea that slaves, women and children are all effectively disposable. So the freedom of one slave would be a threat to the whole of Roman society, which makes Onesimus' self-emancipation so problematic to those in power.

Let's imagine where the idea of freedom takes root for Onesimus. What kind of story from what kind of people could subvert the realities of Roman society and allow Onesimus to believe in the possibility of freedom?

It is sparked by the counter cultural story that Christ has come and Christ has risen! And it is the knowledge that this story of Christ is connected to the liberating stories of Yahweh—which has resonated in the bones of Jewish people for generations. Yahweh, the one who freed people from slavery in Egypt. Yahweh, the God Hagar names in Genesis. Yahweh, who sees and cares for the vulnerable. It is against the backdrop of Yahweh as liberator, and the rumors of a Rabbi claiming to be Son of Yahweh for *everyone*, that allows slaves like Onesimus to imagine a life filled with freedom and hope.

[1] Philemon 1:16

Day after day Onesimus tends to his slave duties with a growing imagination for his freedom and self-worth, bothering him like a rock in his shoe. The good news that this inclusive God has finally come back agitates him as he tries to continue the normal routines of his life. The hopeful thought of liberty disrupts his ability to continue living into the reality of being a slave. Yahweh is the God who liberates the powerless and Christ has come to set the captives free!

He hears more and more about Jesus, the new Rabbi who claims to be The Anointed One and of whom the whole of Jewish community has been waiting for ultimate liberation. Imagine fellow slaves sharing bits and pieces of Jesus' teachings that snap Onesimus from a submissive subservient image of himself and give him imagination for freedom—a new reality of being a child of God. This liberative narrative of including those who are culturally considered the least honorable into the family of God undermines all the stories and systems that keep Onesimus a slave. With a new image of himself as a child of God, there is no way he can participate in someone else's flourishing at the expense of his own. Inspired by a new sense of identity in Christ, he takes new steps in faith, each step away from slavery and toward an identity centered in being cherished by God.

TODAY

Onesimus embodies the liberation made possible by trusting our heart, our personal encounters with God, and our divine imagination. Onesimus' story can remind us of individuals like Dr. Martin Luther King Jr., who made his home in Alabama during the heart of severe Anti-Blackness in the late 50s, to realize a reality only vivid in his imagination. A reality where "little black girls and boys are playing with little white girls and boys" without the violence of racism. There was a yearning in the hearts of Black folks to experience the liberation and flourishing life God intends for everyone—to fully enter into the freedom and unity of the good news. Dr. King took very courageous steps to swim upstream, along with all his contemporaries, against the systemic oppression of his people. They marched against the flow of theological interpretation and cultural norms of the time to live into a new image of freedom.

Both Onesimus and Dr. King invite us to take our personal encounters with God and the promises of God's Kingdom seriously. Jesus invites us to liberation in every way we need it! The transformative, life-giving freedom of the Gospel is for us all, in this present moment of our lives. Many of us have been part of institutions or communities that explicitly or implicitly made us suppress personal truths and forms of identity honored by God. Onesimus gives us a picture of what it looks like to courageously take steps away from those places of oppression and move, toward liberation.

Onesimus' liberation started with some really good news, completely disrupting his reality and provoking him to imagine a new way of being. It reminds us of the same good news—we are all cherished children of God. There are days where every sense of powerlessness and wound in our lives are outshined by new realities of belovedness and a constellation of relationships that remind us just how cherished we are. Our journey to complete healing and hope begins with one faithful step to honor our hearts as we follow the compelling voice of Christ calling us toward freedom.

Alive in Spring

JONATHAN TODRYK

SAND, ACRYLIC, SPRAY PAINT, OIL ON LINEN

Reflect

PAUSE

Sit up straight.

Take a deep breath.

Using the art element (on the previous page), take a moment to reflect on the story.

PONDER

Invite God to speak to you:

I.

How do you think Onesimus felt with a newfound sense of identity walking into the same kinds of relationships and institutions that led to his oppression?

II.

Can you name realities, relationships, people and systems that make you feel like a prisoner to an identity less than a cherished child of God? How would you describe a reality where you are completely liberated?

III.

Have you ever had to break conventional wisdom believing there had to be more for you? What did it cost you? Was the freedom worth the cost?

IV.

When do you feel most free? Who makes you feel most free? What hobbies help you to be your most liberated self? How can you do more of that in your life?

PRAY

God of liberation,
help ignite our divine imagination
to make real subversive freedom
in dark times for ourselves
and for the world.
Amen.

Peter & Cornelius

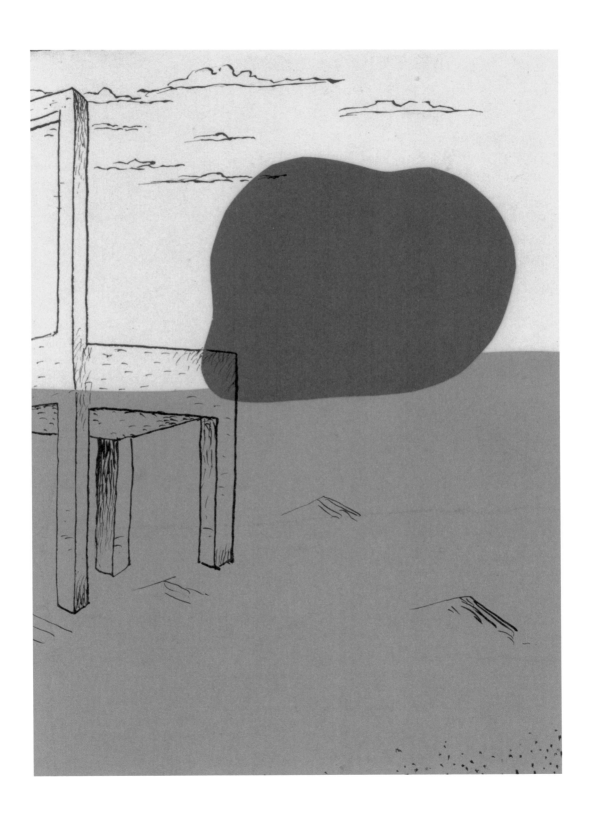

The Story of Peter & Cornelius

SYNOPSIS

Through their shared love of God, Peter and Cornelius, Jew and Gentile, discover an unexpected kinship and purpose with one another.

KEY MOMENT:	FULL READING:
Acts 10	Acts 10-11:18

Read

OUTLINE

We begin with Cornelius. As a centurion of the superpower Rome, he is a person of political privilege, military prowess, and impressive wealth. Despite his lofty status, Cornelius is portrayed as someone who yearns for God and loves God's people.[1] But in the Jews' eyes he is a Gentile: a term used to describe the people whose ethnic, cultural, and spiritual status placed them outside of the bounds of being God's family. Ironically then, Cornelius is on the outside, and he wants to belong to God's family. Contrary to Jew-Gentile constructs, however, God is very aware of Cornelius' presence. God sees Cornelius' love for others and for God, and wants to bring Cornelius into the Divine family. But to do this, God directs Cornelius to seek a kind of person he does not expect—a Jew.

We meet Peter in his prayers and hunger during fasting—a practice linked to religious communities for millennia. In a visionary experience, a blanket falling across the four corners of the earth drops before Peter. The blanket is teeming with creatures. Speaking to one of his needs, God calls on Peter to kill and eat. Peter refuses because many of these animals are "unclean, impure" for a Jew to consume according to Jewish Law.[2] Only Gentiles like Cornelius—those that Jews perceive as not belonging to God's family— eat these things. Peter's need to remain religiously faithful and his need to nourish himself are opposed to each other, but in God's eyes they are not. God suggests something far more radical to Peter than to get hung up on outdated, legalistic frameworks. These animals represented the world and life of the Gentiles, so eating these animals was to enmesh oneself within another people. Peter, however, struggles to accept this. He is unable to sense God's new work of inclusion and embrace. God is turning Peter in his prayer and hunger, not toward God's self per se, but to a kind of person Peter doesn't expect to need—a Gentile.

Eventually, the two who were never supposed to meet come face to face. Despite being unsure as to why they are in each other's company, they both seek to earnestly listen to the other. As Cornelius speaks genuinely, Peter begins to understand that God does not show favoritism, but accepts people from every nation.[3]

As Peter has done before, he narrates the radical, inclusive love of Jesus that embraces all and condemns oppressive powers; a love not even threat and death can break.

But before Peter can finish telling his story, God intervenes. The same Spirit that brought God's loving, inclusive presence into the lives of all Jews now embraces Gentiles.[4] Peter and Cornelius, Jew and Gentile, share in the same love of God—who sees them both as family. Their need to be close to God is transformed by God to need life with *each other*. In one another they encounter and learn from the Divine. This became clear to everyone, enacted in the practice of baptism in the following days. The story of Cornelius and Peter reverberates throughout the rest of history, challenging the faith's understanding of who God calls family, who we will find God working within, and who we call sister, brother, sibling.

[3] Acts 10:34 / [4] Acts 10:44

In our intensely polarized society, it is hard to envision a gathering between two radically different people, let alone envision them calling each other sibling. We, however, cannot forget how unexpected and inconceivable the meeting between Cornelius and Peter was for everyone at the time. The meeting was so unlikely that God needed to build toward it over time—and we can still glean wisdom from their journeys today.

God first prepares Cornelius' and Peters' hearts to meet someone unexpected; God comes to both of them in visions, laying the foundation for their eventual encounter. Then, when they finally do meet, Cornelius and Peter choose to *genuinely listen* to each other despite their different contexts and cultures. They are curious and ask questions of one another: "May I ask why you have sent me?"[5] And finally, as they hear each other's stories and encounters with God, they *trust* in the other's love for the Divine as common ground. It is clear both individuals loved and cherished God wholeheartedly, and they chose to trust that reality in one another. It's only after these things that God's Spirit is revealed and unexpected community is formed.

Maybe that is where we all can start: finding people of faith across race, gender, sexual orientation, class, etc. who are ready to listen to the other because of a shared love for the Divine. Maybe we, too, need inner preparative work to understand why it is difficult to believe God is at work in the other. The unexpected gathering cannot be forced and it isn't instantaneous. It needs Divine power, and it needs to be built on listening and trust. These initial steps, however, can build a needed bridge toward the other who God already sees as family.

UNEXPECTED GATHERINGS

[5] Acts 10:29 NIV

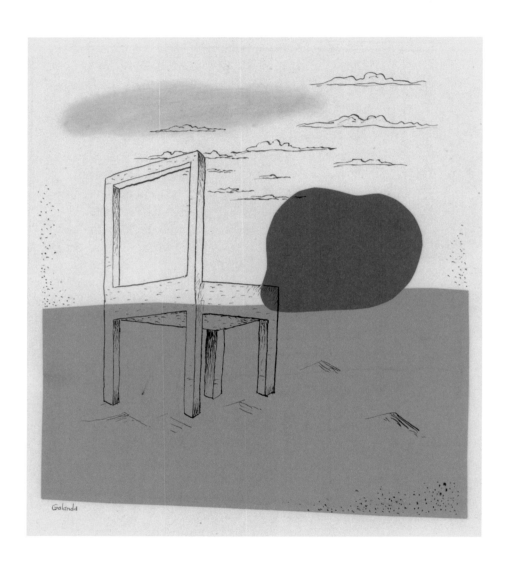

Landscape With a Chair
MIKULÁŠ GALANDA, 1929-1930

INK ON PAPER

Reflect

PAUSE

Sit up straight.

Take a deep breath.

Using the art element (on the previous page),
take a moment to reflect on the story.

PONDER

Invite God to speak to you:

I.

What faith stories have you grown up with that teach
you to call people unclean and impure? Where do
those stories come from? How does this story speak
to those stories you have heard?

II.

Who is the other in your neighborhood; in your
family? What would it mean to listen to the Divine
in their story? How could you start building that
bridge of trust, humility, and bravery toward them?

PRAY

God who loves
us as we are, where we are,
and who shares the Spirit generously.
Generate in us
the ability to see you at work
in the other, in us.
Guide us to each other
into life together at the table of your Presence.
Amen.

Futility / Fleetingness / Meaning of Life

The
Preacher

The Story of The Preacher

SYNOPSIS

This narrative explains what the meaning of life is—or rather, what it isn't. The Preacher has explored every avenue of life, shares his wisdom, and invites us to consider what we should and should not pursue.

KEY MOMENT:	FULL READING:
Ecclesiastes 2	Ecclesiastes 1-12

Read

OUTLINE

The wisdom of Ecclesiastes singes like white charcoal. The unrelenting words of Qoheleth, or the Preacher, reduce to ashes both simple optimism and strict principles of life. Nothing escapes his searing criticisms. Everything is *hevel*—vanity, meaningless, wisps of smoke.

The contested identity of the Preacher (whether Solomon or a different wisdom figure) is not nearly as important as his fiery polemic. He captures the crux of his harangue with a guttural cry: Everything is *hevel*, utterly *hevel*. Commonly translated as "meaningless" or "vanity," *hevel* is much more nebulous than that. The best translation is also its best imagery: wisps of smoke. *Hevel* is fleeting and impossible to grasp. Likewise, the Preacher concludes that life is short and the meaning of life is always shrouded in smoke—a constant enigma. In this smoke, even the surest things in life lose clarity and stability.

In Ecclesiastes 2, the Preacher focuses on three life pillars: pleasure, wisdom, and work. He has summited the pinnacles of life. He has experienced heights very few can identify with and most would toil relentlessly to taste. Nonetheless, he recounts his life in a way the unfortunate and weary find familiar: Everything is *hevel*, utterly *hevel*.

The Preacher has savored pleasure in all its forms: large estates, enviable gardens, slaves and servants, vast flocks, immense riches, endless entertainment, coveted concubines, and satisfaction from his labors. When these were not enough, he amassed more—nothing was denied. He became the greatest in Jerusalem, adored and envied. Nevertheless, he concludes nothing was worthwhile. Pleasure is *hevel*.[1]

[1] Ecclesiastes 2:11

The Preacher has experienced great wisdom, but stifles any optimism bent toward it. The wise and the fool will share the same fate; both will die. What then is the value of wisdom? Furthermore, in the grand scheme of time both sages and fools will be forgotten. The universe does not care whether one life is wise or foolish. Long before us, the sun rose from the east; long after us, the sun will still set in the west—wholly unphased by the death of one life. Wisdom is *hevel*.[2]

Finally, the Preacher finds much success in work—but, too, says it is futile. The strivings, triumphs, failures, and regrets are in vain. We take none to the grave. Sleepless nights plagued with worries, debilitating years of anxiety, a long and arduous life—where is the value when everyone will return to dust? Even if we pass the fruits of our labors to our successors, who knows what will happen to our fortunes and their lives? The rich and the poor, the successful and the failures are equal before death. Success is *hevel*.[3]

And, so, the Preacher chases after every human desire imaginable. But, ultimately, he concludes to chase after these things—pleasure or wisdom or work—is meaningless, akin to chasing after the wind.

TODAY

Vanity of vanities! Everything is meaningless! Nothing matters!

The Preacher seems to scrape the depths of today's buried, dejected cries. How often do we try to fulfill ourselves with luxurious pleasures of all kinds only to find they fall short? How often do we, after experiencing incredible success, find ourselves craving even more success—realizing the goalposts are constantly moving. Life seems so futile before these harsh realities. They thwart our hopes and the ability to dream.

[2] Ecclesiastes 2:17 / [3] Ecclesiastes 2:26

In the midst of these hurricanes and more, it is appropriate and understandable to first read the Preacher's words as a fiery nihilism. But alongside that nihilism, there's another truth simmering beneath the surface. The Preacher looks straight into the eyes of our deepest human cravings, the things that feel so vitally important, and he calls them *hevel*. The Preacher is doing us a favor. He has reached the apex of human possibility in pleasure, wisdom, and work, but concludes they are all futile. He has gone before us so we don't have to; we are invited to let go of our struggles and strifes—knowing these endeavors are meaningless.

Wisdom can come from many sources. In the Bible, we see books like Proverbs and Ecclesiastes offer wisdom from different perspectives. Wisdom, from any source, invites us to engage with a conversation. And so we are left with a choice. We can either spiral down into cynicism or, worse, deny the Preacher's words altogether and continue to tensely pursue pleasures, intellect, and success, believing they will bring us happiness for all eternity. Or, knowing that everything is fleeting, we can relax; we can let go; we can be at ease. We can enjoy simple, divine and earthy gifts in the present. We can trust in God's sovereignty. Here, *hevel* is not something to fear, but a soothing balm that lifts the weight of the world off our shoulders. We can just be. The choice is ours.

Cloud Study (Early Evening)
SIMON DENIS, 1786-1806   OIL ON CANVAS

Reflect

Sit up straight.

Take a deep breath.

Using the art element (on the previous page),
take a moment to reflect on the story.

Invite God to speak to you:

I.

What in your life would the Preacher call *hevel*? Do
you agree?

II.

Is there a time in which you pursued something
with all your might, only to find that it was futile in
the end? How did you respond to that futility?

Righteous and wise God,
help me to pursue
only the good and everlasting,
and let the futile dissipate from my desires.
Show me how to be present with you.
Amen.

The Samaritan Woman at the Well

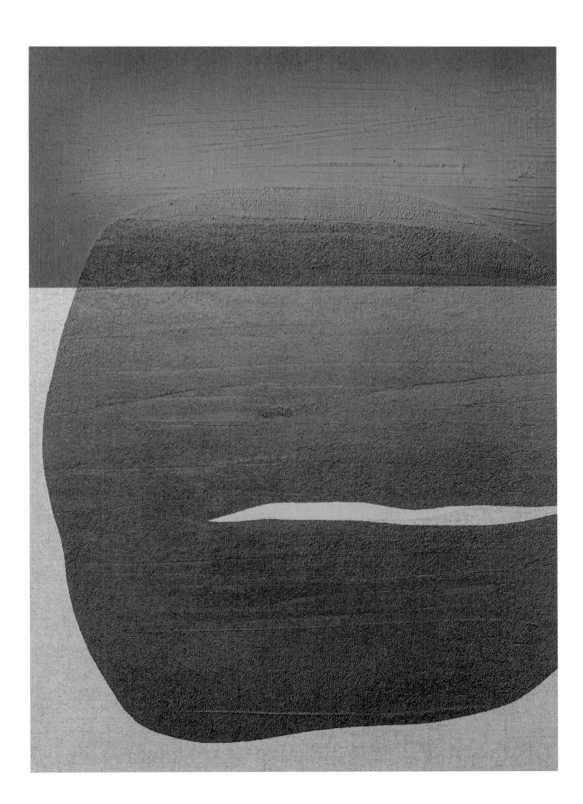

The Story of the Samaritan Woman at the Well

SYNOPSIS

An outcast, alienated woman goes alone to a drinking well for water, and finds Jesus, who offers her much more than she ever could expect—belonging.

KEY MOMENT:	**FULL READING:**
John 4:28-29	John 4:1-42

Read

When Jesus chooses to journey through Samaria, he enters a region fraught with tense interethnic history. His own Jewish people and the people of Samaria are not on friendly terms. They are alienated from one another.

As Jesus sends his disciples off into town and sits down to rest at Jacob's well by himself, he may have been surprised to see a Samaritan woman approach the well—also alone.[1]

The other women from her town may have walked to the well together, earlier in the morning, chatting with one another along the way. They may have sometimes talked about her. What was that one woman's deal, that she had had five different husbands?[2] Perhaps this woman's noontime solo journeys to draw water serve as daily reminders of her alienation from her community.

Likely, people in her village made assumptions about her character that may or may not have been true. In a world where women were not allowed to initiate divorce, surely this woman's marital history says more about her husbands than about her. But she is alone, nonetheless.

ALIENATION / BELONGING

If Jesus is surprised to see her, she must have been even more surprised to see him—and particularly to hear him speak to her. "Give me a drink," he says, initiating conversation.[3] But she knows Jews do not associate with Samaritans.[4] And she knows he must know that as well.

The Jewish people and the Samaritan people shared so much—a common history, a common ancestor Jacob,[5] a belief in a coming Messiah.[6] And yet, these two groups avoided one another. They worshiped in different places—one group in Jerusalem, the other on the mountain where their ancestors worshiped.[7]

Despite this interethnic alienation, Jesus makes himself clear: His offer of living water is for all people. It is not limited to his own ethnic or religious group. His offer is for Samaritans. It is for Samaritan women who are social outcasts even among their own people. *Everyone* belongs.

Jesus' living water is for the lonely and isolated. It's for people who don't have anyone to walk to the well and draw water with. It's for people who have been shamed by their communities.

[3] John 4:7 / [4] John 4:9 / [5] John 4:12 / [6] John 4:25 / [7] John 4:20

Jesus' living water is water that satisfies. Those who drink it, he says, will never be thirsty again. It's water that—as the Greek word could be translated—*leaps up* or *gushes up* into eternal life.[8] It's water that turns alienation into healthy community and belonging. It's water that restores relationships that have turned sour or been broken—among individuals, like the Samaritan woman and the other women in her village, and even among whole communities, like the Jewish people and the Samaritan people.

By the end of the conversation, the Samaritan woman is no longer alone. She is invited to take her place among the true worshipers who worship God in spirit and in truth[9]—a group that includes people of every tribe, tongue, and nation, as the book of Revelation puts it.[10] And now she returns to her village, no longer an outcast but a leader.

"Come and see," she says. And her whole village goes to meet Jesus for themselves.[11]

In our modern world of smartphones and social media, there are more ways to connect with other people than ever before. And yet, many people are lonely. Many people feel isolated and alienated from those around them. We often find it difficult to be present face-to-face with friends and family—our phones always at hand, a ready distraction. Many people want to connect with others but find meaningful relationships difficult to build and sustain.

And like the Samaritan woman, many of us might also feel alienated from others within our personal communities. Perhaps we feel rejected by people we once trusted. We may not be responsible for the rejection, but in any case, we feel alone and companionless when others turn their backs.

Like the Jewish people and the Samaritan people in Jesus' day, we too experience divisions and disconnections among entire groups of people. People of different religious denominations, for example, perhaps worship in different spaces. We are often more ready to consider ourselves superior to others than to seek out connection in humility, openness, and learning—but this only leads to further isolation and detachment.

The discussion between the Samaritan woman and Jesus shows us how a single conversation can go a long way towards changing a person's, or entire group's, experience from abandonment to togetherness. Jesus does not caveat or qualify the woman's belonging; instead she already belongs, simply because she is a child of God.

As Brené Brown writes, "when you get to a place where you understand that love and belonging[...] is not something you have to earn, anything is possible." The woman's conversation with Jesus empowers her to believe that she does belong, which in turn emboldens her to go back to her community to share what she learned about Jesus. As a result, many people believe.

As God's children, we are invited to have conversations like the one the Samaritan woman has with Jesus. We're invited to listen, understand, and celebrate the differences among us—and not to see those differences as reasons to alienate or shame ourselves or others. Instead, our invitation is to see others as deeply loved by God, as God pulls all of us out of our alienation into communities of belonging.

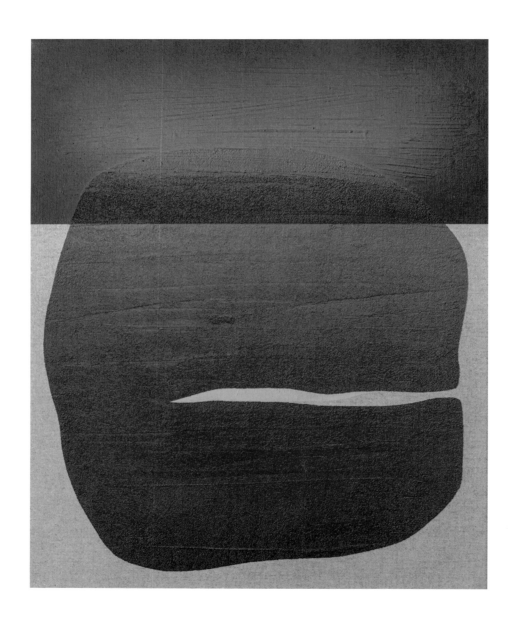

The Well
JONATHAN TODRYK **CONCRETE, ACRYLIC, SPRAY PAINT ON LINEN**

Reflect

PAUSE

Sit up straight.

Take a deep breath.

Using the art element (on the previous page),
take a moment to reflect on the story.

PONDER

Invite God to speak to you:

I.

What is your experience with alienation? Have you
ever felt alienated from community, or been on the
other end, casting others away? Was belonging ever
restored and how?

II.

What kinds of divisions between entire communities do you see in our world? How can you be a
leader, like the Samaritan woman, and invite those
communities to experience belonging?

PRAY

God of the Well,
would you fill us up with
more than what we came for.
Restore our belonging
and mend our divisions
so that we may lead others
to your living water.
Amen.

Serving Present Needs

Stephen

The Story of Stephen

SYNOPSIS

A servant of God and God's people, Stephen, rises to meet the needs of the most vulnerable in his community.

KEY MOMENT:
Acts 6-7

Read

We begin in the middle of Jerusalem, in a time where the apostles' message of Jesus is rapidly spreading across socio-economic divides. Though the apostles are just a handful of ministers, many people pledge their belief in the way of Jesus because of their teachings. Among those people is a Greek-speaking Jew full of faith—Stephen.

Stephen and his fellow believers gather regularly, and their collective daily needs begin to overwhelm the few apostles. A quarrel breaks out. Some of the Hellenistic (Greek-speaking) Jewish people raise against the Hebraic Jewish community leaders that their widows are being overlooked and left food insecure.[1] The felt needs stall the apostles' efforts to preach the word to more people. Who will make sure there is food when they gather? Will there be enough distributed to everyone, even the most vulnerable?

The apostles propose that the people choose seven from amongst them who are full of the Spirit and Wisdom, and appoint them to this responsibility. The community is pleased by this, and they move to appoint Stephen and six others to lead and tend to the needs of others. The word of God spreads even more rapidly.

Time passes in Jerusalem. Stephen serves day in day out, helping the needs of people through wonders and miracles. Though many are in awe, rivaling sects fume and seek to put an end to his efforts by attempting to debate and discredit him. Their efforts fail to stand against his authoritative words and this makes them boil even more. Getting more desperate, they persuade people to lie about Stephen's message. "[He] blaspheme[s] Moses and even God!"[2]

SERVING PRESENT NEEDS

[1] Acts 6:1 / [2] Acts 6:11

The people, elders, and teachers of the law all get stirred up and seize Stephen to put him on trial before the high council. The high priest raises the accusations before Stephen. "Are these charges true?"[3]

All eyes gaze at Stephen in anticipation; his face becomes supernaturally bright.[4]

He berates them with a monologue, emphasizing the stubbornness of their shared Jewish ancestors. From the generations of Abraham to Jacob, Moses, and David, their people have always turned away from the promises and saving work of God. "Must you forever resist the Holy Spirit? That's what your ancestors did, and so do you! [. . .] You deliberately disobeyed God's law, even though you received it from the hands of angels."[5]

A chaotic uproar ensues. Stephen sees this reaction, but full of God's Spirit, turns his gaze from the violent scene, to the heavens above.

"Look, I see heaven open and the Son of Man standing at the right hand of God."[6]

Suddenly, in their anger, they all rush Stephen, drag him out of the city, and cast stones at him.[8] As each stone strikes his body, he utters a prayer before his final breath. "Lord, do not hold this sin against them."[7]

Stephen is buried and many mourn his violent death. Within the same day, a great persecution breaks out all over Jerusalem, and the Jewish believers in Jesus are scattered all throughout Judea and Samaria.[8]

Stephen had no idea the part he was going to play in God's unfolding work. His story, developing in the way it did, was novel and led to an inflection point

[3] Acts 7:1 NIV / [4] Acts 6:15 / [5] Acts 7:2-53 / [6] Acts 7:56 NIV / [7] Acts 7:60 NIV / [8] Acts 8:1

for followers of Jesus. He's considered the first martyr of the church—a Greek-speaking Jew who was responsible for caring for the vulnerable.

Knowing the finitude and mortality of Stephen's life, we can glean a distinct thread woven throughout his story: service grounded in the present. Though he lacked clear foresight of where his life would go, he was always set on present needs—serving both God and people. He heard the needs of the most vulnerable widows in his community, and rose to the responsibility of helping make sure they were met. He saw those seeking (but yet to find) God and performed wonders and signs to help them believe. He received the brutality unleashed by his accusers, but returned compassion towards their violence and petitioned God for the forgiveness they needed.

So often in our modern world, we are fixated on the future, and, as a result, disconnected from what we can do today. But, like Stephen, we don't know what will happen to us tomorrow. We can, instead, live with a focus of serving present needs in our world. Theologian Henri Nouwen describes this present serving, "Our humanity comes to its fullest bloom in giving. We become beautiful people when we give whatever we can give: a smile, a handshake, a kiss, an embrace, a word of love, a present, a part of our life...all of our life."

How can our actions reflect the same value of serving others, *today*? When we look around right now, who do we see in need? Like Stephen, we may never see the complete realization of our services to the world; but by accepting this reality, we give ourselves permission to be *fully* human—finite and beautiful. Here, we embrace our fragility and release to an eternal God our plans for tomorrow. God's cosmic work is constantly unfolding and we are invited to serve, here and now in this generation.

GEORGE CATLIN, 1846-1848

OIL ON CANVAS

Reflect

PAUSE

Sit up straight.

Take a deep breath.

Using the art element (on the previous page),
take a moment to reflect on the story.

PONDER

Invite God to speak to you:

I.

Where do we see the needs that the world presents
to us today? What can we do to be more like Stephen, rising to meet those needs—both physical
and spiritual?

II.

Are there moments in your life's story in which your
actions to meet present needs have ultimately connected to God's eternal healing work?

PRAY

God over all needs,
help me to see like you see,
and have eyes open
to present needs.
Grant me the resolve
to serve the vulnerable
and those who persecute me.
For only you know the eternal story fully,
so that I may be fully human.
Amen.

God's Surprising Care & Justice

Tamar

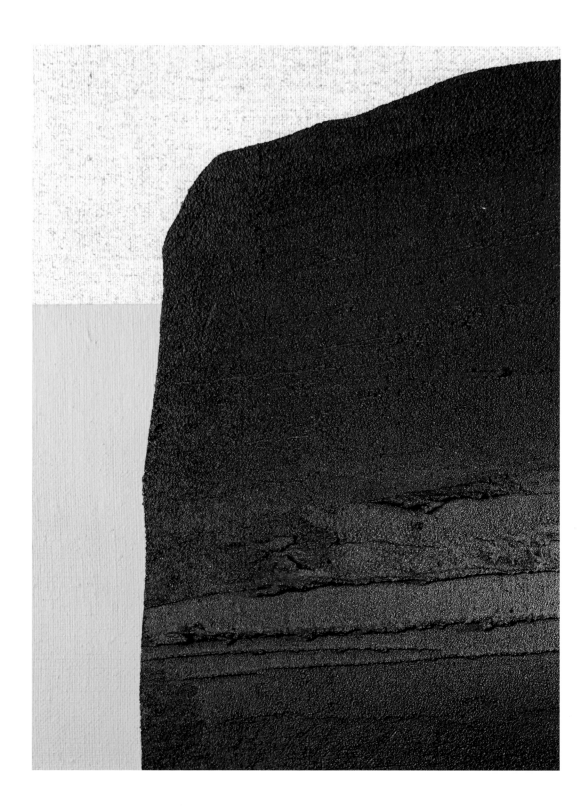

The Story of Tamar

SYNOPSIS

Tamar is caught in a cycle of tragedy and neglect, but she takes a risk to ensure justice for herself and ultimately writes her own great legacy.

KEY MOMENT:
Genesis 38

Read

Tamar is a Hebrew woman who marries Er, the oldest son of Judah, who is one of Joseph's brothers. We don't know much about Er except that he is unjust and immoral in the eyes of God, and so he dies.[1] As is customary, Judah has his next oldest son, Onan, marry Tamar as a surrogate. But because Onan knows that any child he has with Tamar would be his brother's, he refuses to get her pregnant. God considers this unjust and immoral as well, and so Onan also dies.[2]

Judah has now lost two sons and Tamar has lost two husbands. Judah's role as patriarch requires him to protect Tamar and give her a place in his family, but he worries if he marries his last son, Shelah, to Tamar, Shelah would also die. Thinking of his son alone, Judah sends Tamar back to her father's household to live as a widow until Shelah has grown up. Judah has no intention of letting Tamar marry Shelah, but maybe this lie could buy him some time.[3]

This is where the story gets interesting. Tamar is smart; she knows the injustice Judah is doing to her. Without children or a husband, she would have no promise of protection after her father and father-in-law died. Tamar certainly could have sat back and accepted her situation; no one would have blamed her. But instead, in the face of Judah's failure to protect her, she decides to take a huge risk to protect herself. After all, what did she have to lose?

Tamar hears Judah would be making a trip through her area to shear his sheep. Jumping at the opportunity, Tamar disguises herself with a veil and waits along the road. Sure enough, as Judah passes by, he doesn't recognize her. Instead, he propositions her, promising to send her a sheep later as payment. Seeing another opportunity, Tamar accepts and requests that as collateral, he gives her his seal, cord, and staff—also forms of his identification.[4]

Time passes and word spreads that Judah's widowed daughter-in-law is pregnant, the father unknown. This is an offense punishable by death and Judah sees an opportunity to be rid of Tamar once and for all. He sends for her to be brought out and burned.[5]

Facing death, Tamar makes one final bid for her future. She sends Judah the cord, staff, and seal with a message: "I'm pregnant by the man who owns these."[6] Judah is called out in front of the community and he cannot deny what he has done. Instead, Judah confesses that it is he who is in the wrong, not Tamar. He even acknowledges she is more just, more righteous, than he is. He lets Tamar live and he leaves her alone.[7]

But the most striking part of all? The first of the twins Tamar gave birth to is Perez, an ancestor of David found in the genealogy of Jesus alongside his mother, one of only four women acknowledged.[8] All along, Tamar's future is protected by God, and her legacy is far greater than she could have ever imagined.

[4] Genesis 38:14-18 / [5] Genesis 38:24 / [6] Genesis 38:25 NIV / [7] Genesis 38:26 / [8] Matthew 1:3, Luke 3:33

What can we learn from Tamar's story today? It's unlikely many of us will find ourselves in the same exact situation as Tamar. But we, too, may find ourselves in situations where we feel powerless or hopeless.

Tamar may have initially felt like she had no options, but we can see God was with her, advocating for her from the beginning. God saw the injustice done to Tamar in her first two marriages and by Judah and protected her. Tamar isn't a passive participant in the story. Instead, she is brave and takes an acute risk. When we first read the story, we may think she is simply cunning or conniving. Should we judge Tamar for her deceptiveness? Does God? Looking deeper at the story that unfolds, we catch a glimpse of what God values and who God is.

God cares about injustices placed on those most on the margins in society—in this case, a childless widow. Rather than seeing deceptiveness, God sees Tamar's intelligence and bravery, so much so that Judah publicly acknowledges she was more just and righteous than he. Ultimately, her story is woven into the beautiful story of salvation, being part of the genealogy of Jesus.

From Tamar we can learn to trust God sees our challenges and the injustices done to us—and that God *cares*. We can learn to trust that even when we feel we are without an advocate, God is advocating for us. Even amidst the messiness of our lives, God is there, and like Tamar, we can act bravely and cunningly on our own behalf, trusting God's caring justice is there empowering us all along.

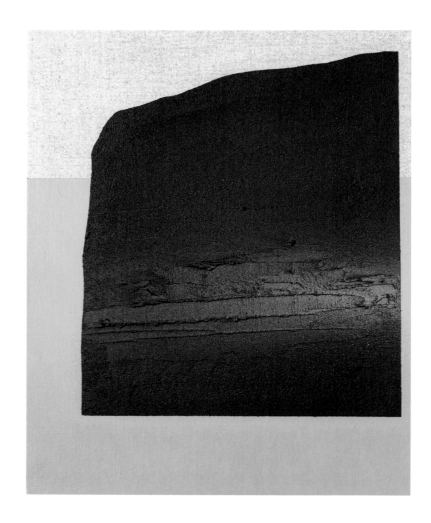

Moving Mountains
JONATHAN TODRYK   CONCRETE, ACRYLIC, SPRAY PAINT ON LINEN

Reflect

PAUSE

Sit up straight.

Take a deep breath.

Using the art element (on the previous page), take a moment to reflect on the story.

PONDER

Invite God to speak to you:

I.

How do we feel as we hear the events of Tamar's story? How can we learn to mourn the brokenness of cycles that keep people victim to their circumstances? How can we gain compassion for those seeking their own justice in an unjust world?

II.

Do you find yourself feeling hopeless or powerless in the face of certain situations? How might God be empowering you to seek care and justice for yourself and for others? How is God present in your challenges?

PRAY

Empowering God,
would you see the reality of our broken world
and care for victims seeking justice.
Would you empower us to make a way for ourselves
against all forms of oppression.
Amen.

Wisdom

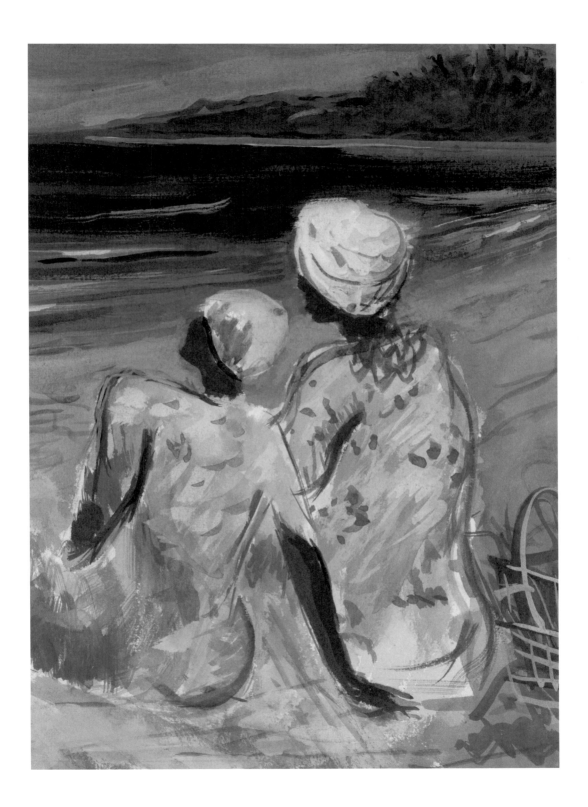

The Story of Wisdom

SYNOPSIS

Wisdom is personified as a woman calling out to those who will listen. She warns of the tragedy that lies in wait for those who reject her.

KEY MOMENT:
Proverbs 1:20-33

FULL READINGS:
Proverbs 1, 3:13-20, 8, 9

Read

OUTLINE

Imagine yourself as an ancient Israelite. You walk through the dusty marketplace, filling your basket with wheat loaves for tonight's dinner. A choir of donkeys bray in the streets, and sellers try to make themselves heard over the pack animal voices. The soft chink of silver coins drawn from purses adds some snare to the bazaar symphony.

Then, you hear a new voice. It's coming from the public square, a dozen paces past the stalls. A woman's voice rings clear against the chaos of the marketplace haggling. This woman speaks with authority. She wants everyone to hear. She demands attention in such a way that you must choose: listen to her or ignore her.

What will you do?

The Book of Proverbs is a collection of sayings, likely compiled for the training of young men in the royal courts. Its overarching theme is learning wisdom by listening to the lived experiences of those who have gone before us.

This first chapter introduces us to a truly beautiful character. Her name is Wisdom. She is the poetic personification of God's own wisdom. In chapter one, she is portrayed as a woman calling out in the streets. She makes her address in a very public place, where the city leaders typically hold court.

In verse 23 we get a snapshot of her heart. She longs to bare her soul to those who would listen. She wants to share the secrets of the universe with those who would heed her advice.[1]

The verses following are her warnings. She invites us to meditate on how destructive it is to shun wisdom. The poetic imagery is that of building a relationship. The foolish build relationships with her only when they are desperate, and they ignore her when they don't quickly understand her benefits.[2]

Wisdom feels this.

She feels the pain of being turned to only when situations are dire. She is not naïve. She understands the manipulative ways people try to take advantage of her resources without truly caring for her. Wisdom hates this. She is hurt when people try to use her only when it's convenient for them.

She asks us to listen to her even when life is going well—when her words don't seem to make that big of a difference. Just as we ought not to seek our friends' company only when we are in good spirits, we should not seek wisdom only in times of disaster. In verse 26, we see the harsh image of wisdom laughing at fools' destruction.[3] This is the reality of our universe. Wisdom does not work when prac-

ticed at the last minute. If we wait too long to build our relationship with her, even God's divine Wisdom will not prevent our self-imposed destruction.

In the last verse of the chapter, we see Wisdom's compassion yet again. She reaches out with a warm embrace to anyone who would build a relationship with her. She offers deep peace to those who would choose to speak with her.[4]

Wisdom teaches us how to approach the rest of the Book of Proverbs. In this book, we may find pieces of advice that sound good but are not immediately necessary. For instance, sayings that encourage us to be diligent or listen to our elders. While we may not need to put that Proverb into practice now, how we interact with it builds our relationship with Wisdom. This applies not simply in the Book of Proverbs, but stands for all the wisdom that we find throughout life. Wisdom is calling to us. She wants to speak.

[1] Proverbs 1:23 / [2] Proverbs 1:24-25 / [3] Proverbs 1:26 / [4] Proverbs 1:33

Take some time to meditate on the metaphor of Wisdom as a woman who wants to have conversations with us. This is a sharp contrast to the way our academic system has taught us to read most scientific or historical non-fiction. Proverbs introduces this character to show us that wisdom is not an intellectual resource we bank up in order to pull out an encouraging one-liner when we need help. Wisdom, instead, is someone that should be talked to and consulted with like a caring mother who wants the best for us.

In our world, this picture of wisdom is very bad for business. A large portion of our economy thrives off of people wanting the low-effort, mindless, most pleasurable solution to everything. But this is the scheme of folly—bombarding us with quick-fix platitudes and promises as a ploy to get us to want more, need more, and buy more things. These messages feel good to hear in the moment, but we know something deeper that can fulfill us. We already hear Wisdom's voice. Calling out to us. Yet amidst the bombarding messages, it is so easy to ignore her.

Then, at the brink of breakdown, we might turn to God and ask for advice. This conditional affair breaks Wisdom's heart. Why do we wait so long before speaking with Wisdom who has been calling for us this whole time?

The invitation of Proverbs 1:20-33 is to practice wisdom even amidst the little things. Wisdom, just like a relationship, is something that takes effort and practice. Take a moment and think of some pieces of wisdom that may be useful in life. Consider moments of screen time or media consumption in the past week. Consider our relationships—with friends, family, and the earth. Are we in regular conversation with Wisdom about these things and more? In everything Wisdom calls out to us; it is our choice to listen.

On the Beach
VICTOR LAREDO, 1935-1943   ACRYLIC

Reflect

Sit up straight.

Take a deep breath.

Using the art element (on the previous page),
take a moment to reflect on the story.

PONDER

Invite God to speak to you:

I.

What makes it hard to listen to wisdom?

II.

How has wisdom led you to safety and ease within
your life?

III.

Think of one practical piece of wisdom you can im-
plement this week. Use that to grow your relationship with Wisdom.

PRAY

God, I want your wisdom to permeate
every aspect of my life.
Help me hear Wisdom's call,
And deliver me from all the voices
that encourage me to live foolishly.
I want to live a life of thriving,
And learn to interact in
the universe as you intended.
Bless me with your wisdom.
Amen.

The Woman Who Anoints Jesus

The Story of The Woman Who Anoints Jesus

SYNOPSIS

A woman breaks an alabaster jar of perfume onto Jesus' head; to the others in the room it is wasteful and foolish; to Jesus, it is generous and beautiful.

KEY MOMENT:	FULL READING:
Mark 14:1-9	Mark 14:1-26

Read

The story begins with the chief priests and teachers of the law secretly plotting to arrest and kill Jesus. They have had enough of this so-called Messiah and are ready to put an end to him.

Jesus, meanwhile, reclines at the table of Simon the Leper. Suddenly, an unnamed woman enters the home. Eyes dart towards her as she pulls out an alabaster jar of expensive perfume—worth an entire year's wages. She breaks it and pours it all over Jesus' head. His hair soaks in liquid as the fragrance fills the room.[1]

The woman's startling act shakes everyone. Many in the room become resentful and indignant, and talk down to her. "Why this waste of perfume? It could have been sold for more than a year's wages and the money given to the poor."[2]

Historically, jars of perfume were intended as dowry gifts. So, there she is, an unnamed woman, not only giving up her potential for a future marriage and security, but receiving the full blunt force of mockery and disgust. All gazes are upon her. She is exposed and alone.

Yet still, despite experiencing all of this dismay, the woman *chooses* to act. She knows her status as an unmarried woman and she knows she is breaking every cultural norm, but she breaks the jar anyway. It is a moment of courage.

Upon hearing the deafening insults of the crowd, Jesus steps in and defends the woman. "Leave her alone. Why are you bothering her? She has done a beautiful thing to me."[3] The woman's act is immediately validated. Jesus, aware of his impending death, sees the woman's actions as preparation for his burial. "She did what she could."[4] In Jesus' eyes, instead of being wasteful, the woman is seen as *generous*. The woman sees Jesus as worth *everything*. She holds nothing back and generously gives, quite literally, all that she has to Jesus.

Instead of unruly or unjustifiable, the woman's act is seen as *beautiful*. Translated as *kalos*, in the original Greek—Jesus sees the woman's act as more than just an aesthetic decision; it is imbued with goodness, virtue, ethics, and morality.

Jesus continues by asserting that the woman's actions will be declared throughout the world. This single act, he says, will reverberate throughout history wherever the gospel is preached.[5] The woman's story begins in a place of exposure, being seen as disturbing and foolish—it ends with her story being seen as worth sharing as a model of generosity and beauty for generations to come.

[3] Mark 14:6 NIV / [4] Mark 14:8 NIV / [5] Mark 14:9

Looking at the story of this unnamed woman, we see what generosity looks like. While the others in the room saw the woman's actions as inherently wasteful, since it could have been given to the poor, the woman understands what true generosity is: an overflow of our loving relationship with God and Creation. Giving is a *good thing*, but when we choose to deduce charity or altruism to merely a transaction or practicalities—like the others in the room—we lose out on the full picture of what generosity is.

The woman's story invites all of us to consider where our acts of generosity stem from. Do we give because we feel obligated, shamed, or forced? Is generosity just another thing to do on our checklist of "good" human behavior? Or, worse, do we give because it "looks good", choosing to virtue signal but not actually give in good faith.

Rather, the woman's story asks us to give because of something deeper—a kinship with others, a love for God, a desire for all of creation to thrive. When we give from these places, it might look funny, awkward, or troubling to others. It might subvert expectations; we might even be judged. But Jesus sees these acts for what they are: fully, wholly generous.

Jesus shows the woman and people in the room that generosity is more than simply a "nice thing". It is *beautiful*. It is *kalos,* in the original Greek, an outward sign of inward goodness. When we act like the unnamed woman we participate in something holy and beautiful.

As we reflect on our lives today, we are invited to bend towards generosity knowing God is generous with us. Like the woman, a single action of kindness might echo throughout the world, throughout history, for generations after us.

A Forest Floor with Roses and a Butterfly

JOSEF LAUER

OIL ON CANVAS

Reflect

Sit up straight.

Take a deep breath.

Using the art element (on the previous page),
take a moment to reflect on the story.

PONDER

Invite God to speak to you:

I.

When was the last time someone was generous with
you? What did it look, sound, smell, taste, and/or
feel like?

II.

Where can you be generous?

III.

Where does your generosity stem from? How can it
be more beautiful?

PRAY

God of beauty,
thank you for all of who you are.
Teach me the fullness of generosity.
Show me where I can
participate in your generous spirit.
Help me see *kalos* all around me.
Amen.

ALABASTER

TYLER ZAK
Product & Branding Director

DARIN MCKENNA
Content Editor & Coordinator

SAMUEL HAN
Art Director

GRACE SUSILO
Layout Designer

TAMI CHIPECO
Assistant Editor

BRYAN YE-CHUNG
Co-Founder, Creative Director, Cover Image

BRIAN CHUNG
Co-Founder, Managing Director

WILLA JIN
Finance & Talent Director

EMALY HUNTER
Operations & Customer Experience Director

EMMA TWEITMANN
Marketing Associate

ALABASTER

WRITERS	STORY
Aaron Dorsey	*Miriam*
Adaobi Ugoagu	*Elizabeth*
Adrian Patenaude	*Boy Jesus*
Bethany McKinney Fox	*Naomi, Nehemiah*
Bryan Ye-Chung	*The Woman Who Anoints Jesus*
Chris Lopez	*Peter & Cornelius*
Darin Mckenna	*Esther, Jonathan*
Dea Jenkins	*Josiah*
Drew Williams	*The Man Born Blind*
Evie Shaffer	*John the Baptist & The Crowd*
Inés Velásquez-McBryde	*Hagar*
Katie McEachern	*Tamar*
Kayla Craig	*Deborah*
Liz Cooledge Jenkins	*The 5000, The Samaritan Woman at the Well*
Mark Fields	*Onesimus*
Mary Day Taylor	*Lazarus, Martha, & Mary*
Matthew Hayashida	*Jethro & Moses, Lydia, Wisdom*
Nicola Patton	*Abigail*
Sabrina Dawson	*Naaman*
Sooho Lee	*The Preacher*
Tamisha Tyler	*The Canaanite Woman*
Teesha Hadra	*Hannah*
Tyler Zak	*Stephen*
Zac Calvo	*The Daughters of Zelophehad, Jacob & Esau*

ALABASTER

ARTISTS	STORY
Alfred Petit	*Lydia*
Bryan Ye-Chung	*Abigail*
Carl Albert Von Salis	*Boy Jesus*
Carl Gustav Carus	*Lazarus, Martha, & Mary*
Claude Monet	*Hagar*
Dea Jenkins	*The Daughters of Zelophehad, Naomi*
Eric Tai	*Elizabeth, Nehemiah, Onesimus*
George Catlin	*Stephen*
Ivan Ozerov	*Miriam*
Jonathan Todryk	*Hannah, The Samaritan Woman at the Well, Tamar*
José María Velasco	*Jethro & Moses*
Josef Lauer	*The Woman Who Anoints Jesus*
Julia Hendrickson	*Josiah*
Julia Signe	*The Canaanite Woman*
Kamisaka Sekka	*The 5000, Jacob & Esau*
Martin Johnson Heade	*John the Baptist & The Crowd*
Max Jensen	*Deborah*
Michelle Radford	*Esther*
Mikuláš Galanda	*Peter & Cornelius*
Samuel Han	*Jonathan*
Simon Denis	*The Preacher*
Thomas Moran	*The Man Born Blind*
Victor Laredo	*Wisdom*
Winslow Homer	*Naaman*

ENDNOTES

THE 5000

• Stewart, Danté. Shoutin' in the Fire: An American Epistle. Convergent Books, 2021.

ABIGAIL

• Rosenberg, Marshall B. Non-Violent Communication: A Language of Life: Create Your Life, Your Relationships & Your World in Harmony with Your Values. Puddle Dancer, 2003.

ESTHER

• Artwork Image produced by Evan Taylor Studio, www.evantaylorstudio.com

THE MAN BORN BLIND

• Brown, Brene. Daring Greatly: How the Courage to Be Vulnerable Transforms the Way We Live, Love, Parent, and Lead. Penguin Random House Audio Publishing Group, 2017.

ONESIMUS

• King, Martin Luther. I Have a Dream. HarperOne, 1991.

THE SAMARITAN WOMAN AT THE WELL

• Hai, Roxanne. "Being Vulnerable about Vulnerability: Q&A with Brené Brown." Blog.ted.com, 16 Mar. 2012, https://blog.ted.com/being-vulnerable-about-vulnerability-qa-with-brene-brown/comment-page-2/#:~:text=When%20you%20get%20to%20a,to%20earn%2C%20 anything%20is%20possible. Accessed 29 Apr. 2022.

STEPHEN

• Nouwen, Henri. Life of the Beloved: Spiritual Living in a Secular World. Crossroad Publishing, 1992.

CONTINUE THE CONVERSATION

www.alabasterco.com